World History
Made Simple

Ruth Beechick

COPYRIGHT © 2006 by Ruth Beechick

For information about other Mott Media publications visit our website at www.mottmedia.com.

ISBN 0-88062-073-0
Printed in the United States of America

Contents

ILLUSTRATIONS

Author's Preface

Long ago, in 1961, I read a book that changed Christian thinking in our times. It was *The Genesis Flood* by Henry M. Morris and John C. Whitcomb. This was a true landmark book since it started the powerful movement of scientists who now work to show that the Earth is "young," only a few thousand years old as the Bible taught all along. I owe a great debt to Morris and Whitcomb and to many of the scientists who accepted their challenge to work on a truly biblical science in the years following 1961.

That book raised for me the question that if scientists show a young Earth, how does history fit into that time frame? History books typically tell of a long prehistory of ape-men and of slowly developing language and agriculture. This evolutionary wording creeps into even the writings of Christians because the view is so entrenched in our society. But the Bible shows Adam farming and talking with God in the very beginning, and it shows Noah farming immediately after the Flood. So I could easily discount those evolutionary guesses about mankind's slow development. But the dates typically given for early Sumer and the beginning of Egypt are bigger problems.

Thus began a long journey of studying how history might fit into the biblical time frame. The scientists at first were willing to add a few thousand years to the Bible genealogies, but with closer Bible study more and more of them would not stretch the literal wording even that much. I discovered that Isaac Newton wrote, "The Egyptians make their history to be older than the world itself." I discovered other historians from the early 1900s and several recent historians all with the same idea of trying to shorten the typical history of early civilizations. These works are cited here in the annotated bibliography, and all are helpful in various ways. My chronology leaves a few holes of uncertainty where scholars disagree, but these are minor now in the total sweep of history as the Bible shows it.

This book is an attempt to condense for today's students my journey from 1961, and to pull together in readable form

what I see at this time to be the best and most biblical view
of world history. I explain how our history got mixed up in the
first place and how the Bible is the best tool for straightening
it out. Although this is aimed at teenage students, anyone can
read the sweep of history here and skip over the questions
and assignments.

Ruth Beechick
Golden, Colorado, 2006

Teacher Introduction

Who can use this course? Anybody from about fifth grade up through high school and later. You can plug it in anytime between other curriculum materials and books you are using for history. Students who know a lot of history will find that this helps them tie their knowledge together in meaningful fashion. Children with less history knowledge will gain a framework for fitting in their future learning.

Adults and teens who want a sweeping view of history can simply read the chapters, omitting the assignments. Homeschoolers and others using this for study can take time for the assignments, which consist mostly of trying to pull the main history idea from each story. There are forty-two sub-sections, so you could take two to three months to go though this, working on it almost daily.

For best results, do chapters 1 to 4 sequentially without a break, rather than scattering them through a year or more. So take a recess from whatever other history you are using. When you get back to other history, the students will have fuller understanding of it. They will be able to fit their studies into a time frame and to better evaluate events of history by Bible principles.

Homeschoolers can take a recess also from language studies to make time for this. This unit involves reading, listening, discussing, writing, spelling, vocabulary, and thinking, so you get plenty of language integrated with this history.

How to Use Chapter 1 ● ● ● ● ● ● ● ● ● ●

Students can work on this **individually**, by using the discussion questions in their own ways. It helps to read the questions first and then answer to themselves as they read through the story or after they read it.

For **groups**, use any of the six lesson plans below. For variety, use different plans on different days. Plan 3 is an interesting idea that people probably do not think of as often as the others. It helps children listen intently to stories that are read orally.

PLAN 1. Parent or one child reads a story aloud, then asks the questions for everyone to answer and discuss. Look back in the story for answers whenever necessary.

PLAN 2. Children read silently, then one person asks the questions and all answer and discuss them.

PLAN 3. Read the questions aloud first, perhaps assigning certain questions to certain children. Then read the story aloud while the children listen intently for the answers. After the story let them answer each question in turn.

PLAN 4. If your children already know a story well, as happens with some Bible stories, try the questions first. If they can answer, then you could move on to whatever follows.

PLAN 5. If a child likes writing, let him read the story and write answers to the questions. Then let him choose one or more of the questions to bring up for family discussion.

PLAN 6. Children skim-read to find an answer and read it aloud directly from the story. You can do this either after reading the full story or before reading it.

Some of the sections have notebook assignments following. These will help students review and summarize the history.

How to Use Chapters 2 to 4 ● ● ● ● ● ● ●

As with chapter 1, students could work **independently** or the stories could be read aloud in a family **group**. Follow with the notebook assignments.

After finishing chapter 3, students will have in their notebooks a written summary showing the sweep of history through the early times, the kingdom of Israel, and the Gentile kingdoms. They should have a good picture of the connected flow of history.

A brief chapter 4 finishes the world's history by telling of the kingdom of Christ. The Bible tells this future history as well as telling past history.

How to Use Chapter 5 ● ● ● ● ● ● ● ● ●

This chapter delves more thoroughly into dating issues. It is not part of the sequential sweep of history, so you could use these sections anywhere in your school-ing and study them not necessarily in order. They are for serious history students. The table of contents lists the topics in Chapter 5 to help you select what you wish to study.

BIBLE VIEW

The Bible-oriented picture in this course shows that God is in charge of history. God sets up kings and brings them down while He works out His plan. History accord-ing to the Bible has **purpose**, and it is **linear**, leading somewhere. It leads to God's predetermined end. This view of history contrasts with pagan views and their theories of recurring cycles, and it contrasts with the evolutionary view with its fictional past and its random future.

Modern historians search for "laws" of history in the sense that scientists search for laws in the physical world. Karl Marx, for instance, taught that his economic law drives all of history. But his system fails everywhere it is tried. Edward Gibbon studied the Roman Empire and developed his laws of how empires fall. But em-pires do not follow his laws. The Bible stories here show that biblical principles drive history. Sin came into the world, and since then all of history has been a struggle between good and evil. This constant struggle *produces* history. We see that struggle everywhere, in the past and in the present. Catastrophic "acts of God" also af-fect history.

STORY APPROACH

This course uses stories to connect together the running stream of history. Stories tell how history began in the first place. Stories tell how each kingdom fell to the following kingdom. Thus students learn to connect everything meaningfully, rather than trying to get the proper order by memorizing dates. This course downplays the use of numerous dates. Instead, it shows how to use a few dates meaningfully.

Stories of early times come directly from the Bible, the only true source for that history, the primary source. Later stories follow the history of the world as it is laid out in prophecy in the book of Daniel. That total stream of history runs all the way from creation to the kingdom of Christ. This way, students can wrap their minds around the history of the world. All past history learning and all future learning can fit into this framework.

The history stories here show two major principles: 1) the linear sweep of history, and 2) God's control and purposes through history.

1

Early Times

Creation

Directions: Read the creation story from its primary source, the Bible. Use either the shortened version below or the full version from Genesis 1:1 to 2:3. This creation portion of the Bible is easier to read than most other portions. The King James Version (KJV) is mid-third grade reading level according to some rating systems. For instance it says "bring forth grass," and a modern version may say "produce vegetation." Several plans for using the discussion questions are in the introduction. Notebook assignments follow the story.

For Discussion ● ● ● ● ● ● ● ● ● ● ● ● ● ●

1. How many days did God use to create everything?
2. On which day was the sun created? (Look back in the story whenever necessary to find answers.)

3. On which day was light created?
4. What could that light be before the sun? (See Revelation 22:5 for a possible answer.)
5. On which day were plants created?
6. How long did plants have to wait for the sun? Could each day, then, stand for a long age?
7. Was man made in the image of God? Were animals made in the image of God? Can you name some things people can do that animals cannot do?

Genesis 1:1 In the beginning God created the heaven and the earth.

3 And God said, Let there be light: and there was light.

5 And God called the light Day, and the darkness he called Night. And the evening and the morning were the first day.

6 And God said, Let there be a firmament in the midst of the waters, and let it divide the waters from the waters.

8 And God called the firmament Heaven. And the evening and the morning were the second day.

9 And God said, Let the waters under the heaven be gathered together unto one place, and let the dry *land* appear: and it was so.

10 And God called the dry *land* Earth; and the gathering together of the waters called he Seas: and God saw that *it was* good.

11 And God said, Let the earth bring forth grass, the herb yielding seed, *and* the fruit tree yielding fruit after his kind, whose seed *is* in itself, upon the earth: and it was so.

13 And the evening and the morning were the third day.

16   And God made two great lights; the greater light to rule the day, and the lesser light to rule the night: *he made* the stars also.

19   And the evening and the morning were the fourth day.

21   And God created great whales, and every living creature that moveth, which the waters brought forth abundantly, after their kind, and every winged fowl after his kind: and God saw that *it was* good.

23   And the evening and the morning were the fifth day.

25   And God made the beast of the earth after his kind, and cattle after their kind, and every thing that creepeth upon the earth after his kind: and God saw that *it was* good.

26   And God said, Let us make man in our image, after our likeness: and let them have dominion over the fish of the sea, and over the fowl of the air, and over the cattle, and over all the earth, and over every creeping thing that creepeth upon the earth.

27   So God created man in his *own* image, in the image of God created he him; male and female created he them.

31   And God saw every thing that he had made, and, behold, *it was* very good. And the evening and the morning were the sixth day.

Genesis 2:1   Thus the heavens and the earth were finished, and all the host of them.

2   And on the seventh day God ended his work which he had made; and he rested on the seventh day from all his work which he had made.

3   And God blessed the seventh day, and sanctified it: because that in it he had rested from all his work which God created and made.

For Your Notebook ● ● ● ● ● ● ● ● ● ● ●

1. Write a statement about God creating the world.

   Save this statement in your notebook. More statements are suggested after the following stories, and at the end of chapter 1 you can use your statements to write a summary of 2000 years of world history. So try to fill each statement with good information. (Sample statements are at the end of the chapter.)

   Here is a short memory verse that gives an important worldview: *In the beginning God created the heaven and the earth* (Genesis 1:1).

   A longer verse with the same message is Exodus 20:11. Research has shown that the rhythm and sound of the KJV make it easier to memorize than other versions.

Geography of Eden

Directions: Read Genesis 2:8-14 below, and do the notebook activities that follow. Genesis is the primary source document and the only one that tells how the world looked before the Flood. For verse 10 it is important to use the KJV, because this faithful translation says that one river parted into four. Hydrologists explain how that water system before the Flood differed from after the Flood. Some modern translations change this verse to match today's water system.

   Genesis 2:8   And the LORD God planted a garden eastward in Eden; and there he put the man whom he had formed.

9   And out of the ground made the Lord God to grow every tree that is pleasant to the sight, and good for food; the tree of life also in the midst of the garden, and the tree of knowledge of good and evil.

10   And a river went out of Eden to water the garden; and from thence it was parted, and became into four heads.

11   The name of the first is Pison: that is it which compasseth the whole land of Havilah, where *there* is gold;

12   And the gold of that land *is* good: there *is* bdellium and the onyx stone.

13   And the name of the second river *is* Gihon: the same *is* it that compasseth the whole land of Ethiopia.

14   And the name of the third river *is* Hiddekel: that *is* it which goeth toward the east of Assyria. And the fourth river *is* Euphrates.

For Your Notebook

Try to draw a map that fits the description of Eden. You will need to use your imagination because this pre-Flood geography does not exist anymore. We cannot know exactly how it was arranged. Label your rivers and countries and the garden. Place a caption on your map so other people will know what they are seeing. Your map will show that the pre-Flood world was very different from today's world. Save the map in your notebook.

2. Write a statement telling a way that Eden's geography was different from today's geography.

It would be a good idea to look at your statement number 1 and try to connect this thought smoothly onto that one. Save all these statements on the same sheet of paper.

Sin in Eden

Directions: Read how sin entered the world and spoiled it. Use a Bible storybook or read the Bible verses below. This reading level is mid-fourth grade. Most modern translations are higher. After reading, use the discussion questions and write statement 3 suggested at the end of the Bible story.

For Discussion

1. Retell the story aloud to your family or teacher. Questions 2 to 5 may help you include all the important parts.
2. What did the serpent do?
3. What did Eve do?
4. What did Adam do?
5. What did God say to the serpent? To the woman? To Adam?
6. Do you ever hear people blame God for bad things that happen instead of realizing that man's sin is responsible for bad things that happen in the world?

Genesis 2:15   And the LORD God took the man, and put him into the garden of Eden to dress it and to keep it.

16   And the LORD God commanded the man, saying, Of every tree of the garden thou mayest freely eat:

17   But of the tree of the knowledge of good and evil, thou shalt not eat of it: for in the day that thou eatest thereof thou shalt surely die.

18   And the LORD God said, *It is* not good that the man should be alone; I will make him an help meet for him.

22   And the rib, which the LORD God had taken from

man, made he a woman, and brought her unto the man.

23   And Adam said, This *is* now bone of my bones, and flesh of my flesh: she shall be called Woman, because she was taken out of Man.

24   Therefore shall a man leave his father and his mother, and shall cleave unto his wife: and they shall be one flesh.

Genesis 3:1   Now the serpent was more subtil than any beast of the field which the LORD God had made. And he said unto the woman, Yea, hath God said, Ye shall not eat of every tree of the garden?

2   And the woman said unto the serpent, We may eat of the fruit of the trees of the garden:

3   But of the fruit of the tree which *is* in the midst of the garden, God hath said, Ye shall not eat of it, neither shall ye touch it, lest ye die.

4   And the serpent said unto the woman, Ye shall not surely die:

5   For God doth know that in the day ye eat thereof, then your eyes shall be opened, and ye shall be as gods, knowing good and evil.

6   And when the woman saw that the tree *was* good for food, and that it *was* pleasant to the eyes, and a tree to be desired to make *one* wise, she took of the fruit thereof, and did eat, and gave also unto her husband with her; and he did eat.

7   And the eyes of them both were opened, and they knew that they *were* naked; and they sewed fig leaves together, and made themselves aprons.

8   And they heard the voice of the LORD God walking in the garden in the cool of the day: and Adam and his wife hid themselves from the presence of the LORD God amongst the trees of the garden.

9   And the LORD God called unto Adam, and said unto him, Where *art* thou?

10   And he said, I heard thy voice in the garden, and I was afraid, because I *was* naked; and I hid myself.

11   And he said, Who told thee that thou *wast* naked? Hast thou eaten of the tree, whereof I commanded thee that thou shouldest not eat?

12   And the man said, The woman whom thou gavest *to be* with me, she gave me of the tree, and I did eat.

13   And the LORD God said unto the woman, What *is* this *that* thou hast done? And the woman said, The serpent beguiled me, and I did eat.

14   And the LORD God said unto the serpent, Because thou hast done this, thou *art* cursed above all cattle, and above every beast of the field; upon thy belly shalt thou go, and dust shalt thou eat all the days of thy life:

15   And I will put enmity between thee and the woman, and between thy seed and her seed; it shall bruise thy head, and thou shalt bruise his heel.

16   Unto the woman he said, I will greatly multiply thy sorrow and thy conception; in sorrow thou shalt bring forth children; and thy desire *shall be* to thy husband, and he shall rule over thee.

17   And unto Adam he said, Because thou hast hearkened unto the voice of thy wife, and hast eaten of the tree, of which I commanded thee, saying, Thou shalt not eat of it: cursed *is* the ground for thy sake; in sorrow shalt thou eat *of* it all the days of thy life;

18   Thorns also and thistles shall it bring forth to thee; and thou shalt eat the herb of the field;

19   In the sweat of thy face shalt thou eat bread, till thou return unto the ground; for out of it wast thou taken: for dust thou *art*, and unto dust shalt thou return.

24 So he drove out the man; and he placed at the east of the garden of Eden Cherubims, and a flaming sword which turned every way, to keep the way of the tree of life.

For Your Notebook ● ● ● ● ● ● ● ● ● ● ●

3. Write a statement telling how sin first entered the world.

Murder in Eden

Directions: Read about the first murder from the Scripture below. Or read this story of Cain and Abel from a Bible storybook. Except for a couple of words like *countenance* and *vengeance*, the reading level on this and the next story ranges in grades 3 and 4. After reading, use the discussion questions. Several ideas for using them are in the introduction.

For Discussion ● ● ● ● ● ● ● ● ● ● ● ● ●

1. Who kept sheep?
2. Who grew crops?
3. Who committed the first murder?
4. What changed God's good world so that murder could happen? (Hint: the answer to this is in the previous story about Adam's sin.)
5. What in this story tells you that Adam and Eve as well as Cain and Abel probably had many other children who are not mentioned in the Bible? (Cain was afraid that "everyone" would slay him. Also, he already had a wife to take with him. See verse 17 of the next section.)
6. Try telling this story in your own words to your family or your teacher.

Genesis 4:1   And Adam knew Eve his wife; and she conceived, and bare Cain, and said, I have gotten a man from the LORD.

2   And she again bare his brother Abel. And Abel was a keeper of sheep, but Cain was a tiller of the ground.

3   And in process of time it came to pass, that Cain brought of the fruit of the ground an offering unto the LORD.

4   And Abel, he also brought of the firstlings of his flock and of the fat thereof. And the LORD had respect unto Abel and to his offering:

5   But unto Cain and to his offering he had not respect. And Cain was very wroth, and his countenance fell.

6   And the LORD said unto Cain, Why art thou wroth? and why is thy countenance fallen?

7   If thou doest well, shalt thou not be accepted? and if thou doest not well, sin lieth at the door. And unto thee *shall be* his desire, and thou shalt rule over him.

8   And Cain talked with Abel his brother: and it came to pass, when they were in the field, that Cain rose up against Abel his brother, and slew him.

9   And the LORD said unto Cain, Where is Abel thy brother? And he said, I know not: *Am* I my brother's keeper?

10   And he said, What hast thou done? the voice of thy brother's blood crieth unto me from the ground.

11   And now *art* thou cursed from the earth, which hath opened her mouth to receive thy brother's blood from thy hand;

12   When thou tillest the ground, it shall not henceforth yield unto thee her strength; a fugitive and a vagabond shalt thou be in the earth.

13   And Cain said unto the LORD, My punishment *is*

greater than I can bear.

14   Behold, thou hast driven me out this day from the face of the earth; and from thy face shall I be hid; and I shall be a fugitive and a vagabond in the earth; and it shall come to pass, that every one that findeth me shall slay me.

15   And the LORD said unto him, Therefore whosoever slayeth Cain, vengeance shall be taken on him sevenfold. And the LORD set a mark upon Cain, lest any finding him should kill him.

16   And Cain went out from the presence of the LORD, and dwelt in the land of Nod, on the east of Eden.

Industries in Nod

Directions: Read about some of the industries in the pre-Flood civilization and use the discussion questions. This story and the rest of the Bible stories here have reading levels from about grades 4 to 6, lower than most modern versions.

For Discussion • • • • • • • • • • • • • • •

1. What industries can you list from the Bible verses?
2. Can you think of other industries the people must have had in order to accomplish the ones listed?
3. On your map of Eden show where Nod might be.

Genesis 4:16   And Cain went out from the presence of the LORD, and dwelt in the land of Nod, on the east of Eden.

17   And Cain knew his wife; and she conceived, and

bare Enoch: and he builded a city, and called the name of the city, after the name of his son, Enoch.

18   And unto Enoch was born Irad: and Irad begat Mehujael: and Mehujael begat Methusael: and Methusael begat Lamech.

19   And Lamech took unto him two wives: the name of the one *was* Adah, and the name of the other Zillah.

20   And Adah bare Jabal: he was the father of such as dwell in tents, and *of such as have* cattle.

21   And his brother's name *was* Jubal: he was the father of all such as handle the harp and organ.

22   And Zillah, she also bare Tubalcain, an instructor of every artificer in brass and iron: and the sister of Tubalcain *was* Naamah.

God's View of Sin

Directions: Read more about the pre-Flood times in the verses below. Then write statement 4 as suggested in the notebook section.

Genesis 6:5   And God saw that the wickedness of man *was* great in the earth, and *that* every imagination of the thoughts of his heart *was* only evil continually.

6   And it repented the Lord that he had made man on the earth, and it grieved him at his heart.

7   And the Lord said I will destroy man whom I have created from the face of the earth; both man, and beast, and creeping thing, and the fowls of the air; for it repenteth me that I have made them.

For Your Notebook • • • • • • • • • • • •

4. Write a statement telling why God brought the Flood.

THE FLOOD AND AFTER

 ## The Flood

Directions: A short version of Noah's Flood story is given below. You can find the full story with all its details in Genesis 6:13 to 9:19. Sometimes Bible storybooks are okay. Other times they show Noah as a Stone Age man and the ark as a rounded toy-like structure. If you use such a storybook, talk about how it differs from the Bible. After reading about the Flood try the discussion questions, and write statement 5 for your notebook.

For Discussion • • • • • • • • • • • • •

1. What did you learn from the story this time that you did not know before?
2. Read aloud a part that tells that the waters covered the whole earth.
3. Can you figure out why people all around the world know tales of a worldwide flood even if they do not have a Bible? (Hint: Remember that everybody is descended from Noah and his family.)

Genesis 6:13   And God said unto Noah, The end of all flesh is come before me; for the earth is filled with violence through them; and, behold, I will destroy them with the earth.

14   Make thee an ark of gopher wood; rooms shalt thou make in the ark, and shalt pitch it within and without with pitch...

17   And, behold, I, even I, do bring a flood of waters upon the earth, to destroy all flesh, wherein *is* the breath of life, from under heaven; *and* every thing that *is* in the earth shall die.

18   But with thee will I establish my covenant; and thou shalt come into the ark, thou, and thy sons, and thy wife, and thy sons' wives with thee...

22   Thus did Noah; according to all that God commanded him, so did he.

Genesis 7:2,3   Of every clean beast thou shalt take to thee by sevens, the male and his female; and of beasts that are not clean by two, the male and female...to keep seed alive upon the face of all the earth...

11   In the six hundredth year of Noah's life, in the second month, the seventeenth day of the month, the same day were all the fountains of the great deep broken up, and the windows of heaven were opened...

13   In the selfsame day entered Noah, and Shem, and Ham, and Japheth, the sons of Noah, and Noah's wife, and the three wives of his sons with them, into the ark;

14   They, and every beast after his kind, and all the cattle after their kind, and every creeping thing that creepeth upon the earth after his kind, and every fowl after his kind, every bird of every sort.

16   ...and the LORD shut him in...

18   And the waters prevailed, and were increased greatly upon the earth; and the ark went upon the face of the waters.

19   And the waters prevailed exceedingly upon the earth; and all the high hills, that were under the whole heaven, *were* covered.

20   Fifteen cubits upward did the waters prevail; and the mountains were covered.

21   And all flesh died that moved upon the earth, both of fowl, and of cattle, and of beast, and of every creeping thing that creepeth upon the earth, and every man:

Genesis 8:1   And God remembered Noah, and

every living thing, and all the cattle that was with him in the ark: and God made a wind to pass over the earth, and the waters asswaged...

13,14   And it came to pass in the six hundredth and first year...in the second month, on the seven and twentieth day of the month, was the earth dried...

18   And Noah went forth, and his sons, and his wife, and his sons' wives with him:

19   Every beast, every creeping thing, and every fowl, *and* whatsoever creepeth upon the earth, after their kinds, went forth out of the ark.

20   And Noah builded an altar unto the LORD; and took of every clean beast, and of every clean fowl, and offered burnt offerings on the altar.

For Your Notebook ● ● ● ● ● ● ● ● ● ● ●

5. Write a statement telling how big the Flood was.

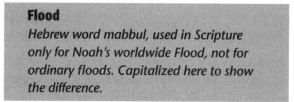

Flood
Hebrew word mabbul, used in Scripture only for Noah's worldwide Flood, not for ordinary floods. Capitalized here to show the difference.

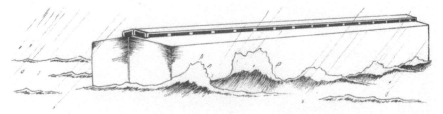

Ark of Noah

Government Begins

Directions: Read the two verses below, and try the discussion questions. At this time in the history of the world, God began the important idea of governments.

For Discussion • • • • • • • • • • • • •

1. If someone murders today, do we call it a crime? (Verse 6 is the beginning of that criminal law.)
2. What does this verse say is the penalty for murder?
3. Who should execute murderers today, government officials or an angry relative of the crime victim? (We *infer* that we need a judge and perhaps a jury to decide if a person really is a murderer, although the verse does not specifically say to do that.)
4. What other command did God give Noah?

Genesis 9:6 Whoso sheddeth man's blood, by man shall his blood be shed: for in the image of God made he man.

7 And you, be ye fruitful, and multiply; bring forth abundantly in the earth, and multiply therein.

Directions: Read this information and then write statement 6 for your notebook.

The Bible tells little about those days immediately after the Flood. We might guess that Noah was in charge at first since he was the head of the family. After the population grew was he the judge and governor? He surely must have taught God's law that it is wrong to kill any human because humans are made in the image of God. Noah probably also taught God's command to multiply in the earth. Did he send out explorers to map the world and find good places to settle?

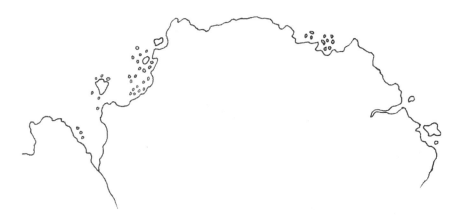

Ancient map showing Antarctica's coastline before it was covered with ice

Most books, except for the Bible, begin their history after the Flood. They often express surprise at how civilization rose up suddenly instead of by long, slow evolution from grunting ape-men to skilled farmers and herders of domesticated animals and builders of cities. But from the Bible it is easy to see how that happened. The Flood survivors remembered a lot from the **pre-Flood** days, so they could teach their children and rebuild quickly. At first people probably were busy just getting food. Later they had time to build houses, find minerals to mine, and other activities that we call civilization. True history shows no evolution. If anything, at times it shows devolution, a downward spiral because people turn away from God.

People in Noah's time held a fresh memory of the great Flood because the old man Noah and his sons told them all about it. Son Shem told everybody to fear God and live for Him instead of living wickedly as people did before the Flood.

But grandson Cush preached a different message, and he became well known for his anti-God preaching among the growing population. He headed up a false religion. He raised his son Nimrod to be a leader in this pagan religion, and he did a good job of that. Nimrod led strong young warriors to kill monster animals that threatened the towns. This made him famous and adulated among the people. So with Cush's preaching and Nimrod's popular leadership, the time was right to get workmen together and begin building a tower for worship of their false gods.

This part of history—from the Flood to the tower of Babel—is missing in history books unless they specifically follow the Bible.

For Your Notebook ● ● ● ● ● ● ● ● ● ● ●

6. Write a statement about civilization arising quickly after the Flood.

pre-Flood	*before* + *Flood*
post-Flood	*after* + *Flood*
antediluvian	*before* + *deluge (flood)*
anti-God	*against* + *God*
(ante and anti have different meanings)	

THE TOWER OF BABEL AND AFTER

The Tower

Directions: Read this story below from Genesis 11:1-9 and use the discussion questions. Or read from your own Bibles. The Bible tells this story only briefly, but it is a significant event in the world's history.

For Discussion ● ● ● ● ● ● ● ● ● ● ● ● ● ●

1. Retell the story in your own words.
2. What materials did the builders use for the city and tower?
3. How could they build a tower so soon after the Flood? (Hints: Think about what the Flood survivors might know, and think about how the population could grow rapidly.)

Genesis 11:1 And the whole earth was of one language, and of one speech.

2 And it came to pass, as they journeyed from the east, that they found a plain in the land of Shinar; and they dwelt there.

3 And they said one to another, Go to, let us make brick, and burn them thoroughly. And they had brick for stone, and slime had they for morter.

4 And they said, Go to, let us build us a city and a tower, whose top *may reach* unto heaven; and let us make us a name, lest we be scattered abroad upon the face of the whole earth.

5 And the Lord came down to see the city and the tower, which the children of men builded.

6 And the Lord said, Behold, the people is one, and

they have all one language; and this they begin to do: and now nothing will be restrained from them, which they have imagined to do.

7   Go to, let us go down, and there confound their language, that they may not understand one another's speech.

8   So the LORD scattered them abroad from thence upon the face of all the earth: and they left off to build the city.

9   Therefore is the name of it called Babel; because the LORD did there confound the language of all the earth: and from thence did the LORD scatter them abroad upon the face of all the earth.

Directions: Read this information and then write statement 7 for your notebook.

Most people gathered in the area that today is Iraq. They named the Tigris and Euphrates rivers there after

two rivers in the pre-Flood world. They worked on walls for the city of Babylon and they worked on Nimrod's tower. It was built with seven towers, one upon another, each smaller than the one below, all filled solidly, and on top was a temple for their false god. People today wonder whether Nimrod's people thought their god would come down to the tower or whether they thought they could reach the gods by

The Tower of Babel may have looked like this.

climbing high enough. Either way, it was a link for them between heaven and earth. But they were linking with false gods. It could be that they were linking with the fallen angels and they called them gods.

Some people believe that there was an astronomical observatory at the top of the tower, because the gods were supposed to be connected somehow with the stars. God intervened again in history. He destroyed the tower and confounded the language. Until then all people spoke the same language, probably the original Hebrew that Adam spoke to God with. Now the people could not understand each other, so they left off building the city.

Ancient Jewish writings say that "fire from heaven" destroyed the tower. Other peoples called it a thunderbolt. The Greeks and Romans both inherited stories of mighty winds that broke apart buildings and even mountains, and forced frightened people to migrate. A Mexican story says that the people who survived this terrible catastrophe lost "their reason and speech." Job 12:20 says that God removes speech and takes away understanding.

Other old documents from around the world say that the planet Jupiter **perturbed** Mercury, pushing it closer to the sun. In its new orbit, Mercury came into close encounter with Earth. Their magnetospheres touched each other and caused a surge of electromagnetic power toward Earth. Ancients called that a thunderbolt, and it affected people's language and thinking. Today when people suffer electric shock or have electrodes applied to their brains, they can lose speech and memory. So that surge of power at Babel could be what affected the brains of the people in Nimrod's time.

For Your Notebook • • • • • • • • • • • •

7. Write a statement about building the tower and about its violent destruction.

perturb	*by means of + troubled movement*
disturb	*utterly + troubled*
turbulent	*troubled (disturbed) + state of*
turbine	*disturbed + rotor (machine)*

After the Tower

Directions: Read the information below and then write statements 8 to 10 for your notebook.

After the tower catastrophe people could not understand each other's languages, so they began to spread out from Babel. Some moved eastward to Asia and others moved westward to Europe, but people could not go very far north because an Ice Age developed shortly after the Flood. The northern peoples had inadequate food and a small population with too much inbreeding, so they developed rickets and other physical problems. They looked deformed and today archeologists call some of them Neanderthal men. That strain of settlers probably died out eventually.

Other settlers moved toward China and India and other far parts of the world, but it took a long time in some cases. The polar ice caps held a lot of water during the Ice Age. So the ocean levels were lower and that left a land bridge across the Bering Strait into North America and land bridges along the strings of islands now off the southeast coast of Asia. Places closer to Babel developed civilizations more quickly.

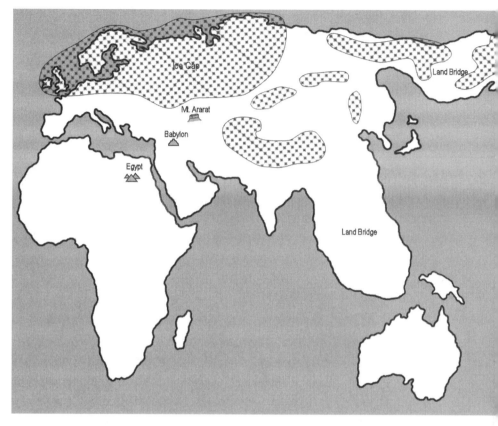

The Ice Age after the Flood

Wherever people went, they took along the pagan beliefs and worship practices that they knew from Babel. That is why pagan religions all over the world have similarities. They have differences, too, because people's memory was impaired along with their languages, and stories naturally become distorted as they pass down through the generations. The account of the tower itself became distorted. The Bible is the only accurate record. God preserved it through the years.

A few stones from the Stonehenge in England

23

The first age had ended with water, the ancients said. And the second age ended with wind, not just ordinary Earth wind, but strong forces from heavenly bodies. So ancient peoples fearfully watched the skies for signs of a coming night, the end of an age. They built structures like the Stonehenge in England in order to study the stars and watch for coming disaster.

Today, many scientists and amateur astronomers have the same fear. They watch the skies for a comet or wayward asteroid to become visible from Earth. Occasionally they announce a sighting and everybody becomes excited and wonders whether the new comet will pass close enough to cause damage.

For Your Notebook ● ● ● ● ● ● ● ● ● ● ●

8. Write a statement that tells what people did after the disaster at Babel.
9. Write a statement about the Ice Age that hindered migration to the north.
10. Write a statement about land bridges that helped migrations.

Sumer

Directions: Read the information below and then write statements 11 and 12 for your notebook.

The area around the tower is called Shinar in the Bible. Archeologists today dig there and find writings from the **Sumerian** civilization. It is not clear exactly who the Sumerians were and where they came from. Their language differed from their neighbors, so we know their writings came after the destruction at Babel. We have recovered many documents from their times, because they wrote on stone tablets that have lasted for thousands of years.

Two tablets are called "King Lists." One contains the names of eight kings said to reign "before the Flood," and the other names ten kings. The Bible does not call anybody a king before the Flood, but it seems that cities in **Sumer** did this to claim that they had kings before anyone else. The writing continued, claiming that after the Flood God sent the kingship down to their city. For a long time nobody knew how to read the numbers on these tablets, and they seemed to say that the kings reigned for many thousands of years each. So history books usually said these tablets were fiction or bragging of the Sumerians. They did not count the tablets as real history. But recently someone figured out how to translate the numbers and they closely fit the life spans of pre-Flood men. So now we know these tablets were real history to the Sumerians, not entirely accurate as the Bible is, but history nonetheless.

Other Sumerian tablets tell their stories of creation and the Flood that included some elements from the true accounts, but many corrupted elements also. Each city had its own pagan god. The city of Ur worshipped the moon god. Abraham grew up in Ur, and a bit later in history God called Abraham out of that pagan environment to be father of a new nation that could teach the whole world about God.

History books used to say that the Greeks or Arabs or somebody later invented writing or the wheel, or even that they invented mathematics, particularly a numbering system based on 60s—a sexagesimal system. Now that archeologists have dug up Sumerian ruins, they say the Sumerians invented these things. They ignore the fact that the wheel and mathematics and many other inventions could have been made even earlier, before the Flood. The pre-Flood world does not enter most history books at all. From the Bible we see that the year originally was a perfect 360 days, and the month exactly 30 days, so from the beginning the sky would be divided into 360 degrees. One indication is that during the Flood five months equaled one hundred fifty days (Genesis 7:11; 8:3,4). If the circle of the Earth and its skies were 360 degrees in the beginning, the sexagesimal system would naturally follow. Our use of dozens and our foot rulers are remnants of that sexagesimal system.

As to writing, we see from the Bible that the pre-Flood people wrote their own history. Then after languages changed at Babel, the groups had to reinvent writing systems to fit their languages. Some groups failed to do that, and they lost the writing skill. This is an example of mankind regressing in their knowledge instead of evolving upward.

Sumer:	*pronounced SOO-mer*
Sumerian:	*soo-MAIR-ee-un*

For Your Notebook ● ● ● ● ● ● ● ● ● ●

11. Write a statement about the people in early Sumer.
12. Write a statement about Abraham.

Egypt

Directions: Read the information below and then write statement 13 for your notebook.

The people who migrated to Egypt found better climate conditions than the northern people. Egypt and surrounding areas were green and well suited for farming and grazing in those days of the Ice Age. The Bible describes it as the "garden of the LORD" (Genesis 13:10). It was not desert as we find today. Explorers may have gone to Egypt earlier, but after Babel, settlers migrated there and began what we call its Old **Kingdom**.

Kings in the Old Kingdom built pyramids. We call the early ones *step pyramids*. They resembled the step towers built in Babylon, but they had no temple on top. Burial tombs in some cases were in tunnels beneath a pyramid, but the king and other royal

An early step pyramid in Egypt

persons were buried in nearby tombs rather than in the pyramids. Temples also were near each pyramid, and a wall surrounded the whole complex of structures. The step pyramid of Zoser (also spelled Djoser) is the first structure we know that was built completely of stone.

A later pharaoh, Cheops, is alleged to have built the Great Pyramid, probably the most famous structure in the world, still standing after thousands of years. This was a true pyramid, not stepped, and it had within it some chambers and hallways. But no mummy has been found in there, or in or under any pyramid for that matter. The Great Pyramid is guarded by a huge sculpture

Great Pyramid and Sphinx guarding it

27

called a Sphinx. It has the body of a lion, which the pagans supposed protected their sacred places, and the face of a king. The face now probably is not the one originally sculpted on it.

Sometime during the Old Kingdom, Abram (also called Abraham) and Lot visited well-watered Egypt with all their flocks. Ancient Jewish writings say that Abraham taught astronomy to the pharaoh. This knowledge helped ancient people produce accurate calendars for their times. They also could align their buildings with true north when they wanted to. Their buildings show that the Egyptians knew a lot of mathematics, geometry, and astronomy.

The kings built palaces and lived in wealth and luxury, but they did not live for the true God that Abraham knew.

kingdom	*king + domain (or condition of)*
freedom	*free + condition*
serfdom	*slave + condition*

For Your Notebook • • • • • • • • • • •

13. Write any statement about the Old Kingdom of Egypt.

The Well-Watered Plain

Directions: Read the Bible story of Lot choosing to live on the plain and use the discussion questions. A short version is below, and the full version is in Genesis 13:1-18.

For Discussion • • • • • • • • • • •

1. Describe the plain that Lot chose.

2. The plain is compared to the garden of the Lord. What garden might that refer to?
3. How does this Scripture describe Egypt?

Genesis 13:2   And Abram *was* very rich in cattle, in silver, and in gold.

5   And Lot also, which went with Abram, had flocks, and herds, and tents.

6   And the land was not able to bear them, that they might dwell together: for their substance was great, so that they could not dwell together.

8,9   And Abram said unto Lot...Is not the whole land before thee? separate thyself, I pray thee, from me: if *thou wilt take* the left hand, then I will go to the right; or if *thou depart* to the right hand, then I will go to the left.

10   And Lot lifted up his eyes, and beheld all the plain of Jordan, that it was well watered every where, before the LORD destroyed Sodom and Gomorrah, *even* as the garden of the LORD, like the land of Egypt, as thou comest unto Zoar.

11   Then Lot chose him all the plain of Jordan...

Directions: Read this information and then write statement 14 for your notebook.

Lot chose the beautiful well-watered plain of Jordan. The Bible says that Egypt, also, was like the garden of the Lord. That certainly is a different Egypt than we know. Today we see water and farming along the Nile River only, but desert in the rest of Egypt. Stretching west from Egypt is the Sahara, the largest desert in the world, and east of Egypt is the Arabian desert.

But the Bible is right to describe Egypt as a garden. Geology studies and satellite images show that there

Drawing of a deer found in the Sahara

was an ancient sea in the Sahara, and a landscape with rivers, lakes, mountains, and valleys. Archeologists dug up tools and other **artifacts** that indicate a history of farming and grazing in the Sahara. They also found over 30,000 rock drawings of forest animals and aquatic animals such as the crocodile and hippopotamus.

There are similar amazing finds east of Egypt, in Arabia. In that desert are a number of dry beds where rivers used to flow. And there is a large empty basin where an inland sea used to be.

Yes, when Lot looked down upon the plain it was well watered just like Egypt. But evil lived in its cities of Sodom and Gomorrah.

For Your Notebook ● ● ● ● ● ● ● ● ● ● ●

14. Write a statement describing the geography of ancient Egypt.

artifact	*skillful item + done*
factory	*doing + place*

SODOM AND GOMORRAH

God's Judgment

Directions: Read the shortened version of the Bible story below, or read all its details in Genesis 19:1-29, and then discuss the questions. If you read in a Bible storybook, be sure to read it also from its primary source in Genesis.

For Discussion ● ● ● ● ● ● ● ● ● ● ● ● ● ●

1. What did the Lord rain upon Sodom and Gomorrah?
2. How do you think scientists might try to explain that rain?
3. The cities and inhabitants were destroyed, and what else was destroyed? (Reread carefully to find this.)

Genesis 19:1 And there came two angels to Sodom at even; and Lot sat in the gate of Sodom: and Lot seeing them rose up to meet them; and he bowed himself with his face toward the ground;

12,13 And the men said unto Lot...we will destroy this place, because the cry of them is waxen great before the face of the LORD; and the LORD hath sent us to destroy it.

15 And when the morning arose, then the angels hastened Lot, saying, Arise, take thy wife, and thy two daughters, which are here; lest thou be consumed in the iniquity of the city.

17 And it came to pass, when they had brought them forth abroad, that he said, Escape for thy life; look not behind thee, neither stay thou in all the plain; escape to the mountain, lest thou be consumed.

24 Then the LORD rained upon Sodom and upon Gomorrah brimstone and fire from the LORD out of heaven;

25 And he overthrew those cities, and all the plain, and all the inhabitants of the cities, and that which grew upon the ground.

26 But his wife looked back from behind him, and she became a pillar of salt.

27 And Abraham gat up early in the morning to the place where he stood before the LORD:

28 And he looked toward Sodom and Gomorrah,

and toward all the land of the plain, and beheld, and, lo, the smoke of the country went up as the smoke of a furnace.

The Great Rift

Directions: Read below about the geography and then finish your statements through number 17.

Brimstone and fire from heaven tore a huge gash through land and sea from Asia down almost to the southern tip of Africa. Maps call it the Great Rift, and it caused destruction far and wide. Lot's plain spewed thick, hot smoke the morning after the disaster. The plain fell low into the new rift. Sodom and Gomorrah disappeared from sight, as did three other cities near them.

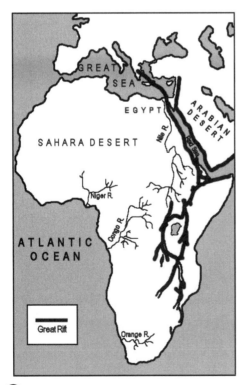

Upheaval on both sides of the rift destroyed more cities. Archeologists call them Early Bronze Age cities, and if they do not believe the Bible they have no idea how all the cities were destroyed suddenly and at the same time. Abraham's hometown of Ur on the Euphrates River was one of them. An ancient poem called *Lamentations over the Destruction of Ur* describes a

cyclone-like storm with fires burning in front. It anni-
hilated the land, people groaned, and bodies lay about
the streets. The land trembled and quaked. The sun rose
not, but shone only as much as a little star.

Egypt, too, was no longer like the garden of the Lord.
Great devastation caused the government to fall, and
the Old Kingdom of Egypt was no more. Lands on either
side of Egypt lost their well-watered landscape and
turned into the Sahara Desert and the Arabian Desert.
The Jordan River flowed into Lot's plain, and it formed
what we now call the Dead Sea, the lowest sea in the
world.

For Your Notebook

15. Write a statement telling what the Great Rift is
    and when it formed.
16. Write a statement about the new geography of
    Egypt.
17. Write a statement telling what happened to the
    political Old Kingdom of Egypt.

    If you read together all your statements so far,
    they should give you a summary of 2000 years
    of world history. Use this outline to remind you
    of the history, and look at it while you write a
    report. You can now connect your thoughts and
    sentences better than the outline does. Add or
    omit any information that you want, and start
    new paragraphs where needed. Save the report
    in your notebook.

Chapter 1—Sample Answer Sentences

1. God created the heavens and the earth in six days.
2. Eden had one river that parted and became four rivers.
3. Adam and Eve ate forbidden fruit and this brought sin into the world.
4. All people became so wicked that God had to destroy them in a Flood.
5. The Flood covered the whole earth, even the highest mountains.
6. After the Flood, people began to farm and build houses and do other activities that they knew about from pre-Flood times.
7. Nimrod and the people built a tower to false gods, and God changed their languages.
8. People could not understand each other's languages, so they spread out from Babel.
9. In Europe they could not go very far north because of the Ice Age.
10. Land bridges in the Pacific helped people cross into North America and into Pacific islands.
11. The Sumerians around Babel are the earliest civilization for which we have found writings.
12. Abraham lived in Sumer, but God called him to a new land.
13. During the Old Kingdom of Egypt they built pyramids.
14. Old Egypt was beautiful and well watered.
15. The Great Rift is a long gash in the earth's crust that formed when God destroyed Sodom and Gomorrah.
16. The Sodom disaster turned beautiful Egypt into mostly desert.
17. The Old Kingdom of Egypt collapsed after God destroyed Sodom and Gomorrah.

Kingdom of Israel

FATHERS OF ISRAEL

Directions: Read about Abraham and study the diagram of Israel. Then write statement 1 on a new page in your notebook.

Abraham. The morning after the terrible catastrophe at Sodom and Gomorrah, Abraham looked down upon the plain and saw smoke arising as the smoke of a furnace.

Soon after that he had a son, Isaac. After Isaac on the chart below are his twin sons. Jacob is the twin important to Israel's history. Israelites often say they worship the God of Abraham, Isaac, and Jacob, naming those first three fathers. God gave Jacob a new name—Israel—and we still call his descendants Israelites. Sometimes we call them Jews, also.

Israel had twelve sons and they headed up the twelve tribes of Israel. Here is a diagram of the early fathers of the Jews.

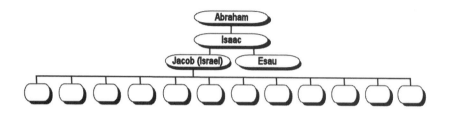

Fathers of Israel

For Your Notebook ● ● ● ● ● ● ● ● ● ●

1. Complete this sentence: The first three fathers of the Israelites were...

   Save the sentence in your notebook. Begin a clean sheet now for the kingdom of Israel. (*Sample answers are at the end of the chapter.*)

Directions: The following story about Joseph and his brothers is directly from the Bible, but shortened. For the full story, see Genesis 37:13-28. This passage and the others in this chapter score about fifth grade reading level. Children may need help with some of the proper names, which likely are not taught in their reading curriculum. And some need help with Middle English words like *hath* and *brethren*. They will meet these later in Shakespeare and other classic literature. After reading the story, write statement number 2 for your notebook.

Joseph and brothers. The Bible tells many stories about these brothers who became the fathers of Israel. They lived turbulent lives, not always getting along with each other, sinning, but believing God and doing good things too. Ten brothers were jealous of Joseph because he was a favorite of their father. This story tells about that.

Genesis 37   And Israel said unto Joseph, Do not thy brethren feed the *flock* in Shecem? Come and I will send thee unto them...Go, I pray thee, and see whether it be well with thy brethren, and well with the flocks, and bring me word again...

And Joseph went after his brethren and found them in Dothan. And when they saw him afar off...they conspired against him to slay him...Come now therefore, and let us slay him, and cast him into some pit, and we will say, Some evil beast hath devoured him...And Reuben said unto them, Shed no blood, *but* cast him into this pit that *is* in the wilderness, and lay no hand upon him...And they took him, and cast him into a pit...

And Judah said unto his brethren; What profit *is it* if we slay our brother, and conceal his blood? Come, and let us sell him to the Ishmeelites, and let not our hand be upon him; for he *is* our brother *and* our flesh...and they drew and lifted up Joseph out of the pit, and sold Joseph to the Ishmeelites [passing merchants] for twenty pieces of silver: and they brought Joseph into Egypt.

For Your Notebook ● ● ● ● ● ● ● ● ● ●

2. Complete this sentence: Joseph's brothers sold Joseph...

   Add this to the sheet with your first sentence. Save all your sentences and at the end of Chapter 2 you can use them to write a summary of the whole history of Israel.

Directions: This amazing story of Joseph is taken directly from the Bible, but is shortened. For the full story, see Genesis 41:1-43. After reading the story, write statements 3 and 4 for your notebook.

Joseph in Egypt. Joseph worked for a government official in the Middle Kingdom of Egypt. Later, in prison on a false charge, he became known as an interpreter of dreams. Then happened a most remarkable story of how he rose from prisoner to second highest ruler in the land.

Genesis 41 And it came to pass at the end of two full years, that Pharaoh dreamed: and, behold, he stood by the river. And behold, there came up out of the river seven well favoured kine and fat-fleshed; and they fed in a meadow. And, behold, seven other kine came up after them out of the river, ill favoured and leanfleshed; and stood by the *other* kine upon the brink of the river. And the ill favoured and leanfleshed kine did eat up the seven well favoured and fat kine. So Pharaoh awoke.

And he slept and dreamed the second time: and, behold, seven ears of corn came up upon one stalk, rank and good. And, behold, seven thin ears...sprung up after them. And the seven thin ears devoured the seven rank and full ears. And Pharaoh awoke, and behold, *it was* a dream. And it came to pass in the morning that his spirit was troubled; and he sent and called for all the magicians of Egypt, and all the wise men thereof: and Pharaoh told them his dream; but *there was* none that could interpret them unto Pharaoh...

Then Pharaoh sent and called Joseph, and they brought him hastily out of the dungeon: and he shaved *himself*, and changed his raiment, and came in unto Pharaoh. And Pharaoh said unto Joseph, I have dreamed a dream, and *there is* none that can interpret it: and I have heard say of thee, *that* thou canst understand a dream to interpret it. And Joseph answered Pharaoh, saying, *It is* not in me: God shall give Pharoah an answer of peace. And Pharaoh [told the dreams].

And Joseph said unto Pharaoh...What God *is* about to do he sheweth unto Pharaoh. Behold, there come seven years of great plenty throughout all the land of Egypt: And there shall arise after them seven years of famine; and all the plenty shall be forgotten in the land of Egypt; and the famine shall consume the land...

Now therefore let Pharaoh look out a man discreet and wise, and set him over the land of Egypt. Let Pharaoh do *this*, and let him appoint officers over the land...And let them gather all the food of those good years that come, and lay up corn under the hand of Pharaoh, and let them keep food in the cities. And that food shall be for store to the land against the seven years of famine...

And Pharaoh said unto Joseph, Forasmuch as God hath shewed thee all this, *there is* none so discreet and wise as thou *art.* Thou shalt be over my house, and...only in the throne will I be greater than thou...See I have set thee over all the land of Egypt. And Pharaoh took off his ring from his hand, and put it upon Joseph's hand, and arrayed him in vestures of fine linen, and put a gold chain about his neck...and he made him ruler over all the land of Egypt.

For Your Notebook ● ● ● ● ● ● ● ● ● ●

Complete each sentence.
3. In Egypt, Joseph rose to be...
4. His main work was to gather up...

It is okay to change the wording of these sentences if you want to. Try to make them good reminders of what you read.

ISRAEL IN EGYPT

Directions: This story of how Joseph saved his family is quoted in shortened form below. The complete version is in Genesis 45:3 to 46:4a. After reading the story, write statements 5 and 6 for your notebook.

Israel moves to Egypt. Down in Egypt, Joseph did his work well. He stored up food in all the cities for seven years, and when the famine came he was in charge of selling food. His father up in Canaan sent the brothers down to Egypt to buy corn. On the first trip they did not recognize their grown-up brother Joseph. This is what happened on the second trip.

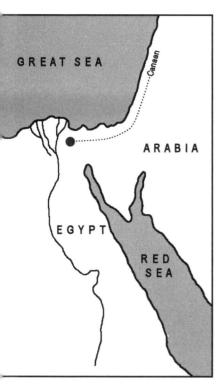

The Israelites move to Egypt.

Genesis 45–46 And Joseph said unto his brethren, I *am* Joseph; doth my father yet live? And his brethren could not answer him; for they were troubled at his presence. And Joseph said unto his brethren... Now therefore be not grieved, nor angry with yourselves, that ye sold me hither: for God did send me before you to preserve life...And God sent me before you to preserve you a posterity in the earth...

Haste ye, and go up to my father, and say unto him, Thus saith thy son Joseph, God hath made me lord of all Egypt: come down unto me, tarry not: And thou shalt dwell in the land of Goshen, and thou shalt be near unto me, thou, and thy children, and thy children's children, and thy flocks, and thy herds, and all that thou hast: And there will I nourish thee...

So he sent his brethren away...And they went up out of Egypt, and came into the land of Canaan unto Jacob their father...And they told him all the words of Joseph, which he had said unto them...And Israel said, *It is* enough; Joseph my son *is* yet alive: I will go and see him before I die. And Israel took his journey with all that he had...And God spake unto Israel in the visions of the night, and said, Jacob, Jacob. And he said, Here *am* I. And he said, I *am* God, the God of thy father: fear not to go down into Egypt; for I will there make of thee a great nation: I will go down with thee into Egypt; and I will also surely bring thee up *again*...

For Your Notebook • • • • • • • • • • • •

Complete each sentence.
5. Joseph's family moved to Egypt because...
6. God promised Jacob (Israel) that...

Directions: Read here about the time of slavery, and then write statements 7 to 10 for your notebook.

Israelites become slaves. The Israelites lived peacefully in Egypt and multiplied and grew into a mighty people. After about three generations, there arose a new king in Egypt who knew not Joseph. The king had a short history memory just as many people do today. He forgot how Joseph had saved Egypt through the famine. He made slaves of the Israelites and ordered that all the boy babies be killed.

In the fourth generation from Jacob, Moses was born and the Egyptian princess rescued him from being killed. During Moses' life the Israelites suffered more and more

Baby Moses

from their cruel taskmasters, and God sent him to ask Pharaoh to let the slaves leave Egypt. Pharaoh said no, he would not let the people go. This began a series of violent catastrophes that affected the whole world. First, God sent a plague that turned water to blood throughout the land—blood-red rivers, bloody ponds, even blood in the water jars. On the other side of the world the Mayans tell the same story, that their river turned to blood. In the far north, Finnish tales tell of the time when red milk sprinkled over all the world. Other stories around the world sound similar.

Scientists try to figure out what happened, and some say that it could have been red hematite (iron ore) dust from the tail of a comet. In Egypt, fish died in the poisoned water so that the water smelled terrible. Frogs then swarmed upon the land and plagued the people. Insects proliferated.

Later, Moses stretched his hand toward heaven and the Lord rained a hail of hot stones, and fire mingled with the hail. That sounds like Earth was deeper into the tail of the comet that earlier had rained red dust. Now it was raining meteorites. Buddhist writers tell of a remote time when a world cycle ended by wind. It began by bringing fine dust, then course dust, then it worked up to large boulders that turned the earth upside-down and destroyed all the mansions in the world. Mexicans have similar stories. Other peoples tell of an age of the world that ended with a rain of fire. It sounds as if the catastrophes reached far beyond Egypt.

Earth passing through the tail of a comet

Through nine plagues Pharaoh still said no, the slaves could not leave. Then came the tenth plague. It included an earthshaking that toppled houses and temples, swallowing some of them. Houses of the slaves could survive because they were made of clay and reeds rather than bricks and stone. Falling walls and buildings brought sudden death into every Egyptian family, and the destruction induced many people to flee along with the Israelites.

Later historians described this destructive event. Eusebius, a third century Jewish historian, wrote of the earthquake by night, so that those who fled from the earthquake were killed by hail and those who sought shelter from the hail were destroyed by earthquake. All the houses and most of the temples fell. St. Jerome, a fourth century Roman historian, wrote that temples were destroyed either by earthshaking or by a thunderbolt. Some later Bible writers also mentioned those earthshakings. (Deuteronomy 4:34, 26:8; Judges 5:4-5; Job 26:11-12; Psalms 68:7-8, 77:15-20, 114:1-8.)

In the middle of the horrible night Pharaoh called Moses and demanded that he get his people out. The Exodus disasters appeared to be worldwide and to be the greatest Earth upheavals since Noah's Flood.

For Your Notebook ● ● ● ● ● ● ● ● ● ● ●

Complete each sentence.

7. A king who knew not Joseph...
8. Moses went to Pharaoh and...
9. After Pharaoh said no, God sent...
10. After ten plagues, Pharaoh...

THE SLAVES ESCAPE

Directions: Read about the end of slavery and write statements 11 and 12 for your notebook.

End of slavery. All those catastrophes left Egypt in chaos, but Pharaoh changed his mind about letting the slaves go. He and his army pursued and caught up with them at the Red Sea. Darkened skies and a violent hurricane-like storm raged all night and made a path in the sea with a wall of water on either side. The slaves crossed on dry land, and when the Egyptians followed, the waters fell back and drowned them all. Now Egypt had no army, no king, and only a devastated land back home.

The Middle Kingdom of Egypt utterly collapsed. And the slaves were at last free. God had prophesied this to Abraham long before. He said that the people would serve another nation and in the fourth generation they would

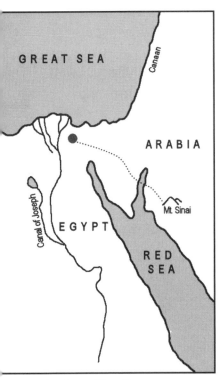

The Israelite slaves escape from Egypt.

return to their promised land. Moses was now the fourth generation from Israel (Jacob), who had moved to Egypt.

Moses wrote the exact date of the Exodus. He said that after 430 years of sojourn, *the selfsame day*, the people of the Lord went out from the land of Egypt. Sojourn refers to a temporary stay in lands not their own, so this sojourn began when Abraham entered Canaan. Then on the selfsame day 430 years later, Moses led the historic Exodus out of Egypt. Later we will see how history writers in King Solomon's time used this Exodus date to count the years of history up to their time.

For Your Notebook • • • • • • • • • •

Complete each sentence.

11. The violent Exodus plagues and the Red Sea drownings caused the collapse...

12. And they helped the slaves...

Directions: This story of Joshua's battle is quoted from Exodus 17:9-14. Read it and then write statement 13 for your notebook.

Battle on the desert. After crossing the Red Sea, the Israelites met warlike Amalekites. Those warriors were fleeing from tidal waves and other destruction in their homeland on the other side of the Arabian Peninsula. Violent upheavals had hit them as well as Egypt.

Exodus 17 And Moses said unto Joshua, Choose us out men, and go out, fight with Amalek: to morrow I will stand on the top of the hill with the rod of God in mine hand...And it came to pass, when Moses held up his hand, that Israel prevailed: and when he let down his hand, Amalek prevailed. But Moses' hands were heavy;

45

and they took a stone, and put *it* under him, and he sat thereon; and Aaron and Hur stayed up his hands, the one on the one side, and the other on the other side; and his hands were steady until the going down of the sun. And Joshua **discomfited** Amalek and his people with the edge of the sword.

And the LORD said unto Moses. Write this *for* a memorial in a book, and rehearse *it* in the ears of Joshua: for I will utterly put out the remembrance of Amalek from under heaven.

After the battle, the Amalekites continued westward and most of them entered Egypt. They looted and killed and destroyed what was not already destroyed by the plagues. In time they set up a capital at Avaris on the eastern edge of Egypt and they ruled cruelly during the time between the Middle and the New Kingdoms of Egypt. They held all power in the north and partial power in the south. History books sometimes call them the Amu or the Hyksos. Later on we will see the end of their history that God promised.

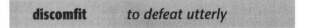

| discomfit | *to defeat utterly* |

For Your Notebook ● ● ● ● ● ● ● ● ● ● ●

13. Complete this sentence: After fighting Joshua in the desert, the Amalekites…

Directions: Read about the earthshaking events at Mount Sinai and then write statement 14 for your notebook. Then read the section on desert wanderings. No assignment follows it.

Mount Sinai. Earth upheavals continued. Another violent event happened at Mount Sinai, which is on the Arabian Peninsula, not the Sinai Peninsula as some maps show.

> **Exodus 19:**18-19 and 20:21   And mount Sinai was altogether on a smoke, because the LORD descended upon it in fire: and the smoke thereof ascended as the smoke of a furnace, and the whole mount quaked greatly. And when the voice of the trumpet sounded long, and waxed louder and louder, Moses spake, and God answered him by a voice...And the people stood afar off, and Moses drew near unto the thick darkness where God *was*.

Smoke rose *up* from the mountain and fire came *down* with the Lord. That was extraordinary. Later, in the time of the judges, Deborah sang about this memorable event. And psalmists wrote more songs about the waters and the mountains of this time.

> **Judges 5:**4b-5   ...the earth trembled, and the heavens dropped, the clouds also dropped water. The mountains melted from before the LORD, *even* that Sinai from before the LORD God of Israel.
> **Psalm 114:**1a,3,4,7   When Israel went out of Egypt...The sea saw *it*, and fled: Jordan was driven back. The mountains skipped like rams, and the little hills like lambs...Tremble, thou earth, at the presence of the LORD, at the presence of the God of Jacob.

People remember those dramatic physical events at Mount Sinai. But it is more important in world history to remember the Ten Commandments that God gave there. Those spread throughout the world, particularly in the western civilizations, and they influenced history more than any other document. Just laws in our nations today have their historic base in those laws of God.

For Your Notebook ● ● ● ● ● ● ● ● ● ●

14. Complete this sentence: We should remember Mount Sinai because...

Desert wanderings. Violent earthshakings always have aftershocks. In this Exodus story, the aftershocks lasted for many years. For forty long years the Israelites camped in the desert and met with more upheavals. One time the earth opened up and swallowed Korah and his followers who rebelled against Moses and God. Deborah sang that the heavens dropped. That indicates darkened skies. In recent history people saw how a single volcano can cause a cloud of dust to circle the earth for a year or more and darken the skies. It was worse after Sinai, because there apparently were many volcanoes then. Some writers point out that the massive eruption of Mount Santorina in the Greek islands occurred about this time.

Egyptian writing by a man named Ipuwer says, "Oh, that the earth would cease from noise, and tumult be no more." This papyrus is now in a museum in the Netherlands. It tells about many of the troubles the Bible mentions, including all ten plagues. On the other side of the world, Mayans wrote of similar trouble. They describe a comet that returned about every fifty years, bringing death to most of mankind.

ISRAEL IN THE PROMISED LAND

Directions: Read the information below and the Bible story that is quoted from parts of Joshua 10:8-14a. Then write statement 15 for your notebook.

Entering the land. The Israelites camped in the gloomy desert for forty years, then began to conquer the promised land. Joshua and the people came to the Jordan River and it stopped flowing. The water stood and rose up in a heap and the people crossed on dry land, something like that day at the Red Sea. Later, the people marched around the walls of Jericho once a day for six days. On the seventh day they marched around seven times, then seven priests blew seven trumpets and the walls fell down. Were those earth upheavals **precursors** to another yet to come?

Joshua won other battles, and then came a battle and a day known around the world. It happened about fifty years after the Exodus.

precursor	*beforehand + to run + agent*
excursion	*out + to run + noun ending*
cursive	*to run (together) + adjective ending*

Joshua 10 And the LORD said unto Joshua, Fear them [armies of five kings] not: for I have delivered them into thine hand...And the LORD discomfited them before Israel, and slew them with a great slaughter...And it came to pass, as they fled from before Israel...that the LORD cast down great stones from heaven upon them unto Azekah, and they died: *they were* more which died with hailstones than *they* whom the children of Israel slew with the sword. Then spake Joshua to the LORD...and he said in the sight of

Israel, Sun stand thou still upon Gibeon; and thou, Moon, in the valley of Ajalon. And the sun stood still, and the moon stayed, until the people had avenged themselves upon their enemies. So the sun stood still in the midst of heaven, and hasted not to go down about a whole day. And there was no day like that before it or after it...

The great stones from heaven again indicate a comet's tail. And a close comet could change Earth's rotation so as to make a long day. No force within Earth itself could do that. Early Spanish explorers in Mexico collected ancient history from the people there, and the writings tell of a remote past when once the night did not end for a long time. So we see a long day on one side of the world and a long night on the other side.

After Joshua's long day there was never another day like it. The gloomy, tumultuous period finally calmed down and Israel finished conquering her promised land.

For Your Notebook ● ● ● ● ● ● ● ● ● ●

15. Complete this sentence: Joshua led the Israel-ites...

Directions: In the land now, God ruled through judges. The judge story below is quoted from parts of Judges 6:1 to 8:28. After reading the story, write statement 16 for your notebook.

Israel under judges. Long before Joshua, God had told Abraham that the people would take the land when the **iniquity** of the Canaanites was full. That time was now. The Canaanites had plenty of time to repent and turn to God, but they did not, so now the Israelites were supposed to kill them all. General Joshua told each tribe what portion of the land to take. Then he died before they finished taking it.

The Israelites failed to kill all the pagan Canaanites, so that led to troubles later on. While Joshua lived, the Israelites served God, and they continued to serve Him during the lives of the elders who had seen God's mighty works through Joshua. Then arose a generation with a short history memory. They knew not the Lord nor the great works He had done for their nation.

With pagans remaining in their midst, the Israelites themselves began to worship idols, and God used heathen nations to judge them because no righteous nations were around. Later, God punished those heathen nations for punishing Israel. Here is a Bible story, much shortened, telling one of the times that God allowed enemies to oppress Israel, and how God sent help after Israel turned back to Him.

iniquity	sin

Judges 6–8   And the children of Israel did evil in the sight of the LORD: and the LORD delivered them into the hand of Midian seven years...And *so* it was, when Israel had sown, that the Midianites came up, and the Amalekites, and the children of the east, even they came up against them; And they encamped against them, and destroyed the increase of the earth...and left no sustenance for Israel, neither sheep, nor ox, nor ass...

And it came to pass, when the **children of Israel** cried unto the LORD because of the Midianites...the angel of the LORD appeared unto [Gideon] and said unto him, The LORD *is* with thee, thou mighty man of valour...And the LORD said unto him, Surely I will be with thee, and thou shalt smite the Midianites as one man...Gideon and all the people that *were* with him, rose up early, and pitched beside the well of Harod: so that the host of the Midianites were on the north side of them, by the hill of Moreh, in the valley.

And the LORD said unto Gideon, The people that *are* with thee *are* too many; bring them down unto the water, and I will try them for thee there…So he brought down the people unto the water: and the LORD said unto Gideon, Every one that lappeth of the water with his tongue, as a dog lappeth, him shalt thou set by himself; likewise every one that boweth down upon his knees to drink. And the number of them that lapped, *putting* their hand to their mouth, were three hundred men: but all the rest of the people bowed down upon their knees to drink water. And the LORD said unto Gideon, By the three hundred men that lapped will I save you, and deliver the Midianites into thine hand: and let all the *other* people go every man unto his place…

And he divided the three hundred men *into* three companies, and he put a trumpet in every man's hand, with empty pitchers, and lamps within the pitchers. And he said unto them. Look on me, and do likewise: and behold, when I come to the outside of the camp, it shall be *that* as I do, so shall ye do. When I blow with a trumpet, I and all that *are* with me, then blow ye the trumpets also on every side of all the camp, and say, *The sword* of the LORD, and of Gideon.

So Gideon…And the three companies blew the trumpets, and brake the pitchers, and held the lamps in their left hands, and the trumpets in their right hands to blow *withal*: and they cried, The sword of the LORD, and of Gideon. And they stood every man in his place round about the camp; and all the host ran, and cried, and fled…

Thus was Midian subdued before the children of Israel, so that they lifted up their heads no more. And the country was in quietness forty years in the days of Gideon.

children of Israel	descendants of Israel (Jacob)

After that night of trumpets and lamps, more Israelites joined the three hundred men and pursued the enemy into their cities, and killed them and their princes. This gave them peace, as the story says, for forty years.

Enemies oppressed, then God delivered. Enemies oppressed again, then God delivered again, over and over throughout the time of the judges. God rescued the people when they turned and cried unto Him.

For Your Notebook ● ● ● ● ● ● ● ● ● ●

16. Complete this sentence: The book of Judges shows that when people turn to God, He will...

   A good memory verse about history is the last verse of Judges (21:25). *In those days there was no king in Israel: every man did that which was right in his own eyes.*

Directions: Read about the golden age when Israel was one united kingdom. Then write statement 17 for your notebook. See if you understand the chart that follows.

United kingdom. All during the period when God chose judges in Israel, every man did that which was right in his own eyes, and that caused trouble. The last judge, Samuel, grew old and the elders said to him, "Now make us a king to judge us like all the nations." Samuel answered that a king would tax them and require their sons and daughters to serve him. A king would take the best fields and give them to his own servants.

But the people insisted, so Samuel anointed Saul to be the first king. David and Solomon followed. These three kings reigned forty years each, and we remember their times as the golden age of Israel. Saul and David were warrior kings. They built up the kingdom to be more mighty than the surrounding nations. Saul helped a pharaoh prince to win Egypt back from the hated Amalekites and that began the New Kingdom of Egypt. Some remnants of the Amalekites lived elsewhere for a while but eventually they were utterly gone as God had promised in Joshua's time.

When Solomon came to the throne in Israel, wars were finished. He reigned amidst peace and great wealth. He had friendly relations with the New Kingdom of Egypt.

For Your Notebook ● ● ● ● ● ● ● ● ● ●

17. Complete this sentence: Under kings Saul, David, and Solomon, Israel was...

A good memory verse about kings in history is Daniel 2:21a. *And he changeth the times and the seasons: he removeth kings, and setteth up kings.*

Egyptian Kingdoms	Catastrophes
	Catastrophe at Babel
Old Kingdom begins	
Kingdom collapses	**Catastrophe** at Sodom
Middle Kingdom begins	
	Israelites move to Egypt
Israelites become slaves	
Kingdom collapses	**Catastrophe** at Exodus
New Kingdom begins	Saul helps a new pharaoh
A princess marries Solomon	Solomon becomes king
Many dealings with Israel	Period of the kings

This chart reviews the history of Egypt and Israel alongside major Earth catastrophes. It shows that Egypt began after the dispersion at the tower of Babel. Then its Old Kingdom collapsed at the judgment of Sodom. Later the Middle Kingdom formed and the Israelites moved there and became slaves. The Middle Kingdom collapsed at the Exodus catastrophes, and the New Kingdom formed by the time of Solomon.

Directions: Read about how the golden age ended, and then write statement 18 for your notebook.

The kingdom divides. In the fourth year of Solomon's reign he celebrated the groundbreaking for the Temple in Jerusalem. Historians recorded in the Bible that this was the 480th year after the people escaped from Egypt (1 Kings 6:1). This piece of timeline shows how the Bible summarizes those years.

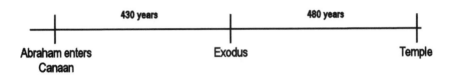

```
|————————————————————————|————————————————————————|
       430 years                    480 years
Abraham enters              Exodus                  Temple
  Canaan
```

Solomon imported fine materials, hired skilled workmen and talented artists, and after years of work they
finished the magnificent Temple. All the congregation of
Israel assembled. Singers and trumpeters and orchestra
filled the air with music. Then Solomon stood up to pray
and the glory of the Lord filled the Temple like a cloud.

Solomon also built palaces for his many wives and
stables for his many horses, and lived in more luxury
than any king of Israel and more than any king of his
time. To support his extravagant life, he taxed the people heavily.

When Solomon died, the old men advised his son
Rehoboam to lift the tax burden, then the people would
serve him forever. The young men advised him to make
the tax burden even heavier. Rehoboam listened to the
young men. So part of the kingdom deserted Rehoboam
and made his brother Jeroboam their king.

Jeroboam reigned over Israel in the north, and Rehoboam reigned over Judah in the south. The golden age
faded, and the kingdoms grew weaker while nearby Assyria and Babylonia grew stronger.

Through the rest of the history of Israel and Judah
some kings did evil in the sight of the Lord, and some
kings did right in the sight of the Lord.

For Your Notebook ● ● ● ● ● ● ● ● ● ●

18. Complete this sentence: After Solomon, the
united kingdom...

Remember you can change the wording of these sentences anytime you want to.

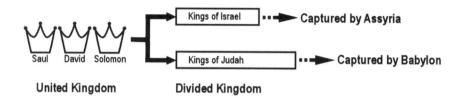

Saul David Solomon

United Kingdom   **Divided Kingdom**

This chart shows the united and divided kingdoms of Israel. First are the three kings of the united kingdom. Then came the split. Assyria captured Israel, and at a later time Babylon captured Judah.

Directions: Read the Bible story below that is quoted from parts of 1 Kings 16:29b to 22:38a. Then write statement 19 for your notebook.

Israel's kings. The Bible tells about an evil king in Israel doing exactly what Samuel had warned that kings would do. Here is the story.

1 Kings 16:29-33 …Ahab the son of Omri reigned over Israel in Samaria twenty and two years. And Ahab the son of Omri did evil in the sight of the Lord above all that *were* before him…And he reared up an altar for Baal in the house of Baal, which he had built in Samaria. And Ahab made a grove [for false worship]; and Ahab did more to provoke the LORD God of Israel to anger than all the kings of Israel that were before him.

1 Kings 21:2-4 And Ahab spake unto Naboth, saying, Give me thy vineyard, that I may have it for a garden of herbs, because it *is* near unto my house: and I will give thee for it a better vineyard than it; or, if it seem good to thee, I will give thee the worth of it in money. And Naboth said to Ahab, The LORD forbid it me, that I should give the inheritance of my fathers unto thee. And Ahab…laid him down upon his bed, and turned away his face, and would eat no bread.

7-16   And Jezebel his wife said unto him, Dost thou now govern the kingdom of Israel? arise, *and* eat bread, and let thine heart be merry: I will give thee the vineyard of Naboth the Jezreelite. So she wrote letters in Ahab's name…saying Proclaim a fast, and set Naboth on high among the people…They proclaimed a fast, and set Naboth on high among the people. And there came in two men, children of Belial, and…witnessed against him…Then they carried him forth out of the city, and stoned him with stones, that he died…And it came to pass, when Ahab heard that Naboth was dead, that Ahab rose up to go down to the vineyard of Naboth the Jezreelite, to take possession of it.

1 Kings 22:37, 38   …the king died [in battle]…and the dogs licked up his blood…

God sent prophets to the evil kings in Israel but they did not turn from their ways. So God let Assyria come and conquer them. The Assyrians relocated the Israelites in other lands and brought strangers to live in their land. The kingdom of Israel was no more.

For Your Notebook ● ● ● ● ● ● ● ● ● ●

19. Complete this sentence: After evil kings in Israel, God let…

Directions: The Bible story about King Hezekiah is quoted from 2 Kings 20:4-11 and 19:35. The story about King Josiah is from 2 Kings 22:1 to 23:25. Read about this final history of Judah. Then do the notebook work suggested at the end.

Judah's kings. After conquering Israel, the Assyrians conquered some cities of Judah. They came to the walled capital of Jerusalem and besieged it. Good King Hezekiah was ill, and the amazing story below tells what happened.

2 Kings 20   ...And it came to pass, afore Isaiah was gone out into the middle court, that the word of the LORD came to him, saying, Turn again, and tell Hezekiah the captain of my people, Thus saith the LORD the God of David thy father, I have heard thy prayer, I have seen thy tears: behold, I will heal thee: on the third day thou shalt go up unto the house of the LORD. And I will add unto thy days fifteen years; and I will deliver thee and this city out of the hand of the king of Assyria...

And Hezekiah said unto Isaiah, What *shall* be the sign that the LORD will heal me, and that I shall go up into the house of the LORD the third day? And Isaiah said, This sign shalt thou have of the LORD, that the LORD will do the thing that he hath spoken: shall the shadow [on the sundial] go forward ten degrees, or go back ten degrees? And Hezekiah answered, It is a light thing for the shadow to go down ten degrees: nay, but let the shadow return backward ten degrees. And Isaiah the prophet cried unto the LORD: and he brought the shadow ten degrees backward, by which it had gone down in the dial of Ahaz [father of Hezekiah].

2 Kings 19:35   And it came to pass that night, that the angel of the LORD went out, and smote in the camp of the Assyrians an hundred fourscore and five thousand: and when they arose early in the morning, behold, they *were* all dead corpses.

That Bible story mentions the sundial shadow as though it were a simple little event. For God it was simple, but He moved the whole Earth to do it. Time speeded forward forty minutes for King Ahaz, and then backward the same amount for his son Hezekiah on the very day that an angel killed all the Assyrian army. When Isaiah earlier had predicted this, he said that God would send a "blast" upon the Assyrians. This loss of their large army weakened Assyria, and they did not bother Judah anymore.

In those days troubles from the heavens occurred about every fifteen years beginning just before Isaiah began to prophesy. The troubles reached other lands too. Men came from Arabia to ask Isaiah to get on his watchtower and tell them when the earthshaking would come again. This earthshaking in Hezekiah's time was the lightest and the last of that series of Earth tremblings. Evidently the orbit of the comet, or whatever it was, moved too far away after that.

One more good king arose in Judah, a young boy named Josiah.

2 Kings 22, 23 Josiah *was* eight years old when he began to reign...and he did *that which was* right in the sight of the LORD...and it came to pass in the eighteenth year of king Josiah, *that* the king sent Shaphan...to the doers of the work, that have oversight of the house of the LORD...to repair the breaches of the house...

And Hilkiah the high priest said unto Shaphan the scribe, I have found the book of the law in the house of the LORD...And Shaphan read it before the king...And the king went up into the house of the LORD, and all the men of Judah and all the inhabitants of Jerusalem with him, and the priests, and the prophets, and all the people, both small and great: and he read in their ears all the words of the book of the covenant which was found in the house of the LORD.

And the king stood by a pillar, and made a covenant before the LORD, to walk after the LORD, and to keep his commandments and his testimonies and his statutes with all *their* heart and all *their* soul, to perform the words of this covenant that were written in this book. And all the people stood to the covenant...

And the king commanded...to bring forth out of the temple of the LORD all the vessels that were made for Baal... and he put down the idolatrous priests...them also that burned incense unto Baal, to the sun, and to the moon, and to the planets, and to all the host of heaven...And he brake down the houses of the sodomites...And he slew all the priests of the high places that were upon the altars... And the king commanded all the people, saying, Keep the passover unto the LORD your God, as *it is* written in the book of this covenant...

And like unto him was there no king before him, that turned to the LORD with all his heart, and with all his soul, and with all his might, according to all the law of Moses; neither after him arose there *any* like him.

Following Josiah, only evil kings reigned in Judah. Neighboring Babylon grew into the superpower, and its king Nebuchadnezzar became king of all kings. He conquered Assyria, and many other lands. He forced Zedekiah to be his puppet king in Judah.

In a later year, Nebuchadnezzar came again and burned the Jerusalem Temple and all the houses, and broke down the city walls. He captured the king and citizens, and transported them to Babylon, leaving only a few poor people to take care of the farmland. This utterly destroyed the kingdom of Judah.

While in captivity the Jews continued to hope in God. Jeremiah prophesied that they would serve the king of Babylon for seventy years and then return to their land.

For Your Notebook ● ● ● ● ● ● ● ● ● ● ●

20. Complete this sentence: After evil kings in Judah...

All your sentences now are reminders of the history of Israel that you have read. Look at them and try to write a summary. Take about two or three paragraphs to tell the beginning of Israel, their move to Egypt and escape from Egypt, then their own kingdom and final fall to Babylon. A summary cannot mention many details. It tries to connect some major ideas.

You should now have a summary of the Early Times and a summary of the Israel times. The next chapter will take you through the rest of the world's history.

Chapter 2—Sample Answer Sentences

1. The first three fathers of the Israelites were Abraham, Isaac, and Jacob.
2. Joseph's brothers sold Joseph to the Ishmeelites and they took him into Egypt.
3. In Egypt, Joseph rose to be second highest ruler in the land.
4. His main work was to gather up food during the good years.
5. Joseph's family moved to Egypt because there was food, and Joseph offered them good land.
6. God promised Jacob that his descendants would come out of Egypt again.
7. A king who knew not Joseph made slaves of the Israelites.
8. Moses went to Pharaoh and asked him to let the slaves go.
9. After Pharaoh said no, God sent plagues to Egypt.
10. After ten plagues, Pharaoh let the people go.
11. The violent Exodus plagues and the Red Sea drownings caused the collapse of the Middle Kingdom of Egypt.
12. And they helped the slaves escape to freedom.
13. After fighting Joshua in the desert, the Amalekites invaded Egypt and ruled them cruelly.
14. We should remember Mount Sinai because God gave the Ten Commandments there.

15.   Joshua led the Israelites into the promised land.
16.   The book of Judges shows that when people turn to God He will help them.
17.   Under kings Saul, David, and Solomon, Israel was united in one kingdom.
18.   After Solomon, the united kingdom split into two.
19.   After evil kings in Israel, God let the Assyrians conquer them.
20.   After evil kings in Judah, God let Babylon conquer them.

3

Gentile Kingdoms

BABYLON

Directions: Babylon was the first of the great Gentile kingdoms, and its king had a dream remembered all through
history. Read here about the dream and then start a new
sheet of paper for your notebook.

Golden age of Babylon. Teenage Daniel was one of
the Jewish captives in Babylon. He and three friends
studied in the king's pagan school, but they remembered
what they learned about God during their childhood
in Judah. King Nebuchadnezzar tested them and found
them to be ten times better than all the magicians and
wise men in his kingdom.

One night King Nebuchadnezzar dreamed something
that troubled him. He awoke and worried, but he could
not remember what the dream was. He called all the
magicians and wise men but none could tell him the
dream or its meaning. Finally somebody brought Daniel
to the king. Daniel asked to have some time. Then he

and his friends prayed and God gave Daniel the answer in a night vision. He returned to the king and gave this answer.

Daniel 2:31   Thou, O king, sawest, and behold a great image. This great image, whose brightness was excellent, stood before thee; and the form thereof *was* terrible.

32   This image's head *was* of fine gold, his breast and his arms of silver, his belly and his thighs of brass,

33   His legs of iron, his feet part of iron and part of clay.

34   Thou sawest till that a stone was cut out without hands, which smote the image upon his feet *that* were of iron and clay, and brake them to pieces.

35   Then was the iron, the clay, the brass, the silver, and the gold, broken to pieces together, and became like the chaff of the summer threshingfloors; and the wind carried them away, that no place was found for them: and the stone that smote the image became a great mountain, and filled the whole earth.

36   This *is* the dream; and we will tell the interpretation thereof before the king.

37   Thou, O king, *art* a king of kings: for the God of heaven hath given thee a kingdom, power, and strength, and glory.

38   And wheresoever the children of men dwell, the beasts of the field and the fowls of the heaven hath he given into thine hand, and hath made thee ruler over them all. Thou *art* this head of gold.

39   And after thee shall arise another kingdom inferior to thee, and another third kingdom of brass, which shall bear rule over all the earth.

40   And the fourth kingdom shall be strong as iron: forasmuch as iron breaketh in pieces and subdueth all *things*: and as iron that breaketh all these, shall it break in pieces and bruise.

42   And *as* the toes of the feet *were* part of iron, and part of clay, *so* the kingdom shall be partly strong, and partly broken.

44   And in the days of these kings shall the God of heaven set up a kingdom, which shall never be destroyed: and the kingdom shall not be left to other people, *but* it shall break in pieces and consume all these kingdoms and it shall stand for ever.

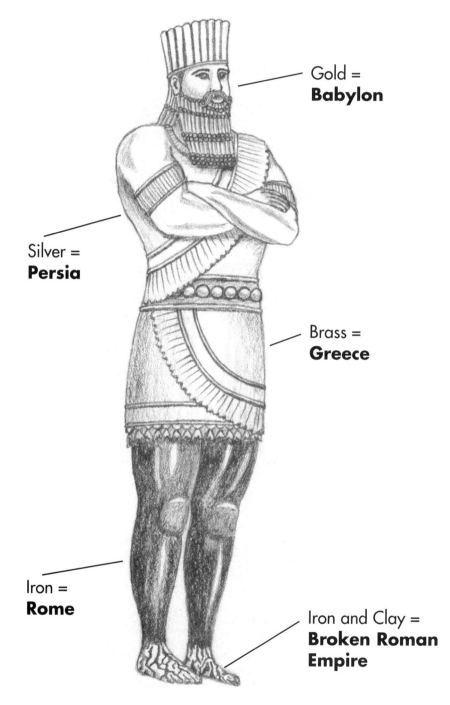

Gold =
Babylon

Silver =
Persia

Brass =
Greece

Iron =
Rome

Iron and Clay =
**Broken Roman
Empire**

Nebucadnezzar's dream image in Daniel 2

The head of gold was Nebuchadnezzar, the king who dreamed the dream. His kingdom **Babylon**, was the gold kingdom, the first of the great **Gentile** kingdoms. Silver was next on the image and it was going to be Persia, which at first was combined **Media** and **Persia**. The brass was going to be Greece. An angel told Daniel those names of the gold and silver and brass kingdoms. The angel did not name Rome, but it is easy for us to see that Rome was the superpower that followed Greece. So Rome was going to be the iron kingdom. It would last a long time, but eventually break into pieces. The feet and toes show pieces of the iron and pieces of clay that will not mix. That is where we live now—with the broken pieces of Rome. Still to come is Christ's kingdom that will smash the image and fill the whole world. It will stand for ever and ever.

King Nebuchadnezzar was proud to be the head of gold. He gave Daniel a high position in the kingdom, and Daniel's friends also. So these captive **Jews** helped to rule in the Gentile kingdom of Babylon.

Babylon:	*today is Iraq*
Medes:	*today are Kurds*
Persia:	*today is Iran*
Gentiles:	*all non-Jews*
Jews:	*from Judah; used interchangeably with Israelites to refer to God's people*

For Your Notebook ● ● ● ● ● ● ● ● ● ●

1. Draw four stepping stones on a full sheet of paper. Make them as large as you can and label them for the four Gentile kingdoms—Babylon, Persia, Greece, and Rome. Save this drawing in your notebook. Later you can place some

words on each stone that will help you remember something about each kingdom.

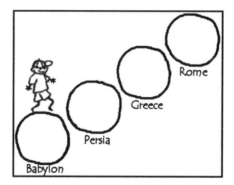

Directions: Read what happened to Babylon suddenly one night. Then carefully work assignment 2 for your notebook.

Fall of Babylon. After Nebuchadnezzar, King Belshazzar ruled in Babylon. Proud Belshazzar felt safe from the enemy who threatened his city. They were digging a trench outside the walls, but Belshazzar thought they could do no harm. He had built extra walls, and he had stored twenty years of food. He also had water, since the Euphrates River ran under the walls and right through the city. King Belshazzar laughed and ignored the enemy.

One night Belshazzar gave a great feast with one thousand nobles and women. He began drinking wine and then called for the gold and silver goblets and bowls that Nebuchadnezzar had stolen from the Temple of the Jews. The merrymakers drank from the ornate holy cups and praised their gods of gold and silver and brass and iron and wood and stone.

Suddenly everybody watched in terror as a hand appeared and began writing on the wall. Belshazzar trembled. What did the words say? Not one of the astrologers and wise men could read the words. Then the queen mother came into the banquet hall and told Belshazzar about wise Daniel who had helped Nebuchadnezzar in the old days.

They called in Daniel and he read the words. He told Belshazzar, "God has numbered the days of your kingdom and it is finished. The kingdom is divided and given to the Medes and Persians."

That very moment the Medes were finishing their trickery. They diverted the river into their trench and it flowed into a lake. Then the soldiers and their general walked in the river bed right under the city walls. Somebody opened gates on the river walls and there the Medes were, quite suddenly inside the city. They easily killed the drunken king. The rest of the city hardly knew they were conquered that night.

For Your Notebook ● ● ● ● ● ● ● ● ● ● ●

2. On the Babylon stone in your drawing write several words to remind you of Babylon. Name persons or items or actions—anything that helps. After you finish all the stepping stones you can use them to tell someone the history of the kingdoms, so choose the best words you can.

PERSIA

Directions: Read about Persia when it was a great power. Then carefully choose some words for the Persian stepping stone in your notebook.

King Cyrus. At first the new kingdom was called Medo-Persia. But in a short time famous King Cyrus of Persia dominated, so we now remember Persia as the silver kingdom.

As soon as Cyrus gained power he **decreed** that the captive Jews could return to their own land. A large company of Jews trekked the long and dusty route to their homeland. They rebuilt houses, and city walls for Jerusalem, and they built the Temple that Nebuchadnezzar had destroyed. The Persians still ruled over the Jews, but the kings were usually friendly to them. Persia grew larger than any kingdom before it.

| **decree** | *a formal order by high authority* |

Xerxes against Greece. An angel told Daniel that the fourth king from Cyrus would be "far richer than they all: and by his strength through his riches he shall stir up all against the realm of Grecia" (Daniel 11:2).

The fourth king, named Xerxes, was the richest king ever. He probably was the king who took Esther for his queen. He often battled with the troublesome Greeks, and one year he decided to conquer the Greek city-states once and for all. He sent an army by land along the coast of the Mediterranean Sea. And he sent ships to row by sea.

The Greek city of Athens received word that Xerxes and his Persian forces were approaching by land and by sea. The citizens assembled at the Parthenon, where

Themistocles stood to speak to them. Other Greek cities were separate little kingdoms. Would they unite with Athens? Would Sparta join? Sparta and Athens both had ships.

Themistocles argued for a strategy of fighting at sea. Farmers and other landowners opposed abandoning the land and trusting to the sea. After a long debate Themistocles won. A league of nearby cities sent their women and children and old people off to safety. They manned their ships, and some land forces too, and prepared to meet the Persians.

The Persians arrived and fighting began. Once a storm accosted the Greek ships for three days and they lost many. Battles followed at sea and on land, with the Greeks often retreating. Persian King Xerxes was happy. His army crossed the land, burning it as they advanced. They came right up to the Parthenon and burned it.

Existing ruins of the Parthenon

Themistocles tried a clever deceit. He sent a Persian friend to King Xerxes to say that the Greek ships were planning to retreat. Xerxes believed that false information, so all night his ships maneuvered to where they intended to cut off the retreat, capture all the Greek ships, and end the war.

By morning the Persians were exhausted. But the Greeks lured them into a narrow strait that led into wider water. Coming through the narrows they met Greek ships, Spartans on the right, Athenians on the left, and Corinthians farther north to guard against a surprise attack there. The front Persian ships slowed as they met the attack. Their own ships from behind jammed into them. There was no room to turn around, and they couldn't backwater either. Up ahead the Greeks rammed into them. They lost ships to the Greeks and they lost ships in the jam.

King Xerxes, watching from a hillside jumped up in fury. But he could do nothing. This famous battle at the island of Salamis ended the Persian westward expansion.

Greek and Persian ships at battle

For Your Notebook ● ● ● ● ● ● ● ● ● ●

3. In the Persian stepping stone of your drawing write several words to remind you of the Persians. They let the Jews return home. They met defeat at Greece. Name people, battles, or anything that will help you remember.

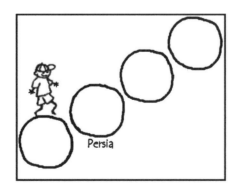

Persia

GREECE

Directions: Probably the greatest conqueror in all of history brought Greece to power. Read his exploits and choose a few reminder words for your notebook.

Invading the Persian Empire. Young Prince Alexander inherited power in Macedonia, which is the northern part of what we now call Greece. He quickly gained power over Greek cities in the south, too.

Then he turned eastward. With his Greek army they manned boats and set out toward **Asia Minor**. After the short crossing, Alexander jumped from a boat and waded ashore before anybody else. He hurled his spear into the beach and claimed his right to Asia. Then he visited the ruins of nearby Troy and traded his shield for one on display there that a guide told him had belonged to the great military hero Achilles. Alexander knew the history of Achilles at Troy because he learned it from his teacher Aristotle.

Alexander and his army then marched through Asia Minor, fighting a Persian army and conquering cities as they went. Some cities they destroyed, massacring and enslaving the people. Other cities surrendered out of fear or because they welcomed Greece as liberating them from the hated Persians.

At Jerusalem the high priest led a delegation to meet Alexander. They surrendered to him in exchange for a promise to spare their city. The Jews were not ambitious for political power, but only wanted to continue their religious worship. The priests told Alexander about the book of Daniel where it said that a mighty king of Greece would stand against Persia. Was Alexander that mighty king?

In Egypt, Alexander managed to get himself pro-claimed king with hardly any bloodshed or cruelty. He ordered a city to be built there and he named it Alex-andria. the first of more than thirty cities named after

him. Then he pressed on to the city of Babylon. In a fierce battle there he almost killed the king he was after, Persian king Darius III. Darius escaped that time, so Alexander forged on to Susa, one of the capitals of Persia. The city surrendered without a fight. He entered the beautiful palace where Queen Esther once lived, and he sat on the throne there. An old friend cried because many

Alexander dashing into battle

Greek soldiers had not lived to see that great moment. In the city, Alexander found treasures that the Persians had looted from Athens long before.

Alexander and his army marched on to the "Persian Gates." That was the name for a high mountain plateau where King Darius could place his army to stop an en-emy from coming down to the capital of Persepolis (per SEE po lis). Alexander outwitted the Persians by split-ting up his army and moving silently at night. His own forces descended a steep and dangerous secret route he had learned of. By morning the surprised Persians found themselves trapped with Alexander at one end of the mountain pass, a second general at the other end, and a third general in the middle. The Persians fought bravely as the Greeks overwhelmed them. This battle of the Per-sian Gates is remembered as the most hazardous and daring mountain campaign in all of history.

The Greeks then entered the city of Persepolis. The king escaped, but he had no time to rescue his treasures. At the palace Alexander found immense riches, taxes collected from all over the world's greatest empire. He now could pay his soldiers for waging war across Asia. He told his troops not to touch the palace, but they could loot the rest of the city.

When the Greeks at last caught up with Darius, a soldier found the great king abandoned in a wagon, stabbed by his own men. Alexander arrived and saw him already dead. This was only four years after he first threw his spear into Asian soil. That was lightning speed for an army in those days. They had crossed Asia Minor and pushed into Asia, taking part of Africa, too, along the way.

Asia Minor	*western tip of Asia where Turkey is today.*
Persepolis	*Persian + city*

Deeper into Asia. Alexander, leader of the brass empire, now confidently ventured north and east through dangerous deserts and mountains, plundering and massacring, and hunting remaining leaders of the Darius regime. He was wounded several times. In one city a comrade seized the Achilles shield from fallen Alexander and protected him, saving his life.

The troops were becoming harder to control as they wearied of war and wanted to go home. Dissenters sometimes were executed. In a drunken rage, Alexander murdered one of his best friends.

After he conquered Asia all the way to the Himalayan Mountains, Alexander turned south toward India. In India, his army would go no further, and he had to head north toward Babylon. On this return trip a portion of his army drowned one night as a desert flash flood caught them sleeping on a flood plain.

Back in Babylon, Alexander increasingly was drunk and ill and eventually he died, not quite thirty-three years of age. Some years later, rumors surfaced that he had been poisoned, but at the time nobody suspected that.

Generals fought over the empire that Alexander built, and eventually they carved it into four parts ruled by four different people. Daniel had predicted that the empire of the "mighty king" that stood up to Persia would be divided toward the four winds of heaven. Alexander had left behind many Greek governors and soldiers. They spread the Greek language and culture throughout his huge area that reached both west and east, that reached both Europe and Asia. Alexander the Great had influenced all future history of the world.

Gold Babylon and silver Persia were fallen, and brass Greece was now the greatest power.

For Your Notebook ● ● ● ● ● ● ● ● ● ●

4. On your stepping stone for Greece write the name Alexander the Great and any other words that will remind you of how the Greek kingdom came to be.

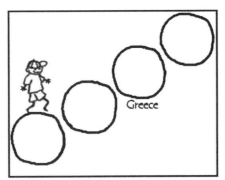

ROME

Directions: Read about the famous people who helped Rome become the greatest power of all. Then work assignment 5a for your notebook.

First triumvirate. While Greece was spreading eastward, a new power was growing in the west. It was Rome. At first they had too many military leaders each doing his own thing. But in time three leaders agreed to a truce and formed a ruling **triumvirate**. That looked peaceful on the surface and it gave each leader time to plot against the others.

Julius Caesar, one of the three, conquered north and west in Europe, going so far as to invade Britain. Crassus, the second, lost his life and his army while fighting in the east. That left Caesar to fight it out with Pompey. Pompey was gaining control over the eastern lands and Caesar's army chased him.

In the east, Egypt was ruled by Queen Cleopatra, a descendent of the Greek ruler who took over that part of Alexander's kingdom. Though only eighteen years old, Cleopatra had learned ruthless ways growing up in a king's family. In some matters she was shrewd enough not to rule as her father had. She lowered taxes and helped her people become prosperous. She learned Egyptian language, and several others, too. In public she dressed like the Egyptian goddess Isis and said that she represented the goddess on earth. This helped her become popular with the Egyptians.

Her capital Alexandria had become the greatest city in the world. It had a museum and a library known far and wide. Its many thousands of books contained all the knowledge in the world, it was said. Scholars from all

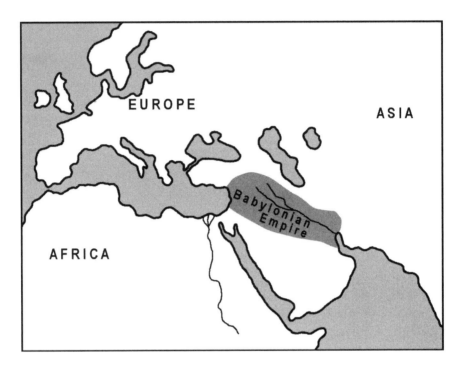

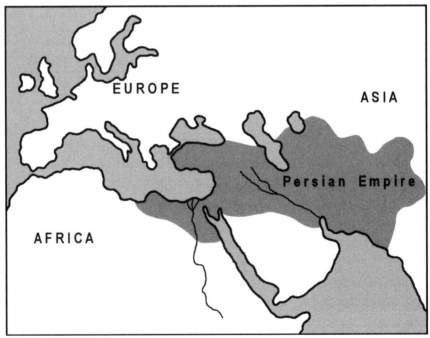

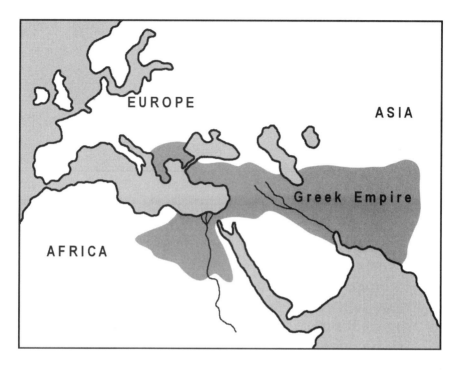

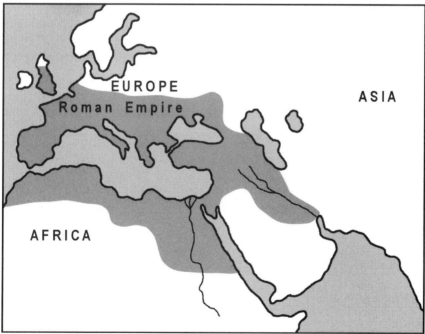

over the Mediterranean world came there to study. Seventy Jewish scholars were invited there to translate the Hebrew Scriptures into Greek. That translation is called the Septuagint, and it still exists today. Alexandria had become the center of Greek learning, taking over that role from Athens.

The city had a beautiful harbor and palaces and temples and entertainment everywhere. Cleopatra had plenty of wealth in Egypt but not a strong military. She knew she must support the winning side in the Roman struggle between Caesar and Pompey. Pompey lost a sea battle and fled to Egypt for refuge. Caesar, pursuing, found himself blocked by Egyptian ships in the harbor, so he burned the ships and then entered the city. The Egyptians helped Caesar but killed Pompey. When Caesar returned to Rome, Cleopatra went with him. She had chosen the winner. For now.

In Rome, some patriotic politicians suspected that Caesar would set himself up as absolute king. They were tired of constant civil war and wanted to get back to a republican form of government that Rome formerly had. Sixty of those senators conspired together and assassinated Caesar. This assassination has become one of the most renowned events in history, and later Shakespeare wrote a play about it.

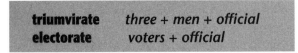

| **triumvirate** | *three + men + official* |
| **electorate** | *voters + official* |

Second triumvirate. After Caesar was killed, his friend Mark Antony, a good orator, incited the people to riot and the assassins fled for their lives. Cleopatra fled too, back to her palace in Egypt. This left Antony to be a member of the next triumvirate.

Antony was in charge of the eastern lands, and he needed the wealth of Egypt to help him expand even farther east, so he sent a message for Cleopatra to meet him. It is said that Cleopatra was very beautiful, as all princesses in ancient stories seem to be. And she was wily. She ignored the first message and kept Antony waiting. She ignored more messages.

Mark Antony holds a map of his empire on three continents. North is at left on this map.

At last she set out to meet him in a barge with a stern of gold, its purple sails billowing in the wind. Her rowers dipped silver oars in time to the music of flute, pipes, and lute. Cleopatra this time was dressed as the goddess Venus, the Roman goddess of love. Rich perfume wafted to the river banks.

After that impressive meeting, Cleopatra gave Antony ships and men and supplies to wage his wars in the east. She married Antony and hoped to become queen of all the Roman lands. Antony let Cleopatra rule Egypt and some other lands too. For Judea, he selected Herod to be ruler.

Back in Rome, a young nephew of Julius Caesar named Octavian gained support from the people and sailed east to fight Cleopatra and Antony. The two were at sea when they met Octavian. They lost that sea battle and fled back to Egypt. Then their troops refused to fight any further.

Whenever the Romans won a war they liked to celebrate through the streets of Rome, parading their trophies in chains before all the people. Neither Antony nor Cleopatra wanted to be humiliated like that, so both committed suicide. That was the end of Greek rulers in Egypt.

For Your Notebook • • • • • • • • • • •

5a. On the Rome stone in your notebook write some important names and words from the first and second triumvirates. Try to leave room for more Roman words.

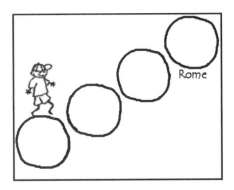

Directions: Christ came into the world, right here in Roman Empire times. Read of that and of many centuries following. Then add about three important words for your notebook.

First emperor. Antony's defeat ended the Roman Republic. From that time it became the Roman Empire, and the first emperor was Caesar's nephew, who took the name Caesar Augustus. He was the very emperor that we read about in the Bible who ruled when Jesus was born. He left Herod in charge of Judea, the same Herod who tried to kill baby Jesus in Bethlehem.

Augustus cleverly made it look like the **senate** had its traditional powers, but behind the scenes he collected all power to himself. The senate consisted of the rich and elite. They were not elected.

For about fifty years in the time of Augustus there was relative peace in the Mediterranean world. The constant civil wars ceased. Jesus who created the world came into the world—the most important event in all of history.

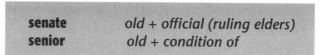

senate	*old + official (ruling elders)*
senior	*old + condition of*

Western and Eastern Roman Empires. The iron Roman Empire lasted longer than any empire before it. Emperor Constantine moved his capital from Rome to Byzantium in the East. He renamed the city Constantinople (now Istanbul in Turkey). After that, the East and West drifted apart and become two. Some people think the two iron legs of the image illustrate this split.

The western part of the empire fell in the mid 400s to various invaders from the north—Huns, Goths, Germans, Vandals, and others. Following that, the broken parts in Europe had a complex history. Christianity continued to spread.

Meanwhile other parts of the world grew pagan civilizations. In the Americas the Olmec, Mayan, and Aztec civilizations rose and fell. China at one time called in her fleet and decided to stay home and defend herself from the strong Mongols and to separate from the rest of the world. They invented printing, iron making, and other advances before people in the West, but they kept that knowledge to themselves. Pacific islands became settled and African cultures developed. Books differ on the dates for all these civilizations, but much of it happened during the times of the Greek and Roman empires.

After the fall of the western Roman Empire, the eastern part lived another thousand years under the name Byzantine Empire. In the 600s, Mohammed came along and his Muslim religion grew into a strong kingdom itself, practically always fighting, and at one time possessing land all the way from India to the Atlantic coast. In what history books call the crusades, Christians fought the Muslims and pushed them back to the Middle East. That long struggle weakened Byzantium and it finally fell to the Muslim Turks a bit before 1500.

This fall of the eastern Roman Empire is the time that books say the Renaissance began. The Renaissance was named for a rising again of the old Greek culture that had moved east to Byzantium and to the Arabs. Scholars now moved from the troubled East back to Europe. The Protestant Reformation of breaking away from the Roman church occurred about this time also.

For Your Notebook ● ● ● ● ● ● ● ● ● ● ●

5b. On the Rome stone add words to help you remember Rome's empire periods.

Directions: Whew! You have been sweeping rapidly through history. Finish the journey here. Then do assignment 5c for your notebook, and choose one of the review assignments also.

Broken Rome. Daniel had said long before that the iron kingdom would break in pieces and subdue all things. The thoroughly broken Roman Empire did exactly that. The Spanish and Portuguese pieces conquered much of Central and South America. The French and Dutch and other pieces ruled most of Africa. Russia took large chunks of land. The British subdued colonies around the globe. People said that the sun never set on the British Empire. Other European pieces likewise subdued peoples until the whole world looked like the feet of the image—strong iron and muddy clay that would not mix.

Most countries in the Americas gained back their freedom, but they retained the languages and much of the culture from the pieces of the old Roman Empire. Some other parts of the world also retained Roman culture. Right up to World War II, the European nations still colonized much of the world. During the war, Allied leaders made plans for freeing all the colonies.

About the first nation to be established was Israel, then occupied by Britain. Israel had a well trained army that had been fighting in the war alongside the British, and they declared that they would be a sovereign nation the very day that the British pulled out. The change of government took place at midnight, and fourteen minutes later five Arab nations attacked to try to wipe out all the Jews. They outnumbered the Jews thirty to one, but God was with Israel and they prevailed.

It took about fifty years for European nations to gradually release other colonies and help them begin to govern themselves. That brings the history up to the 2000s, to the iron and clay pieces that do not mix and often fight each other. But there is yet a final ending to the image.

For Your Notebook ● ● ● ● ● ● ● ● ● ● ●

5c. Finish the Rome stone of your drawing with one or two key words about broken Rome.
6. Now use all four of your stones to try to connect the history of the Gentile kingdoms. What

great king in Babylon dreamed about the kingdoms? How did Persia take over Babylon? How
did Greece take Persia, and Rome take Greece?
Continue by describing broken Rome. Explain
this to your mother or somebody, and add or
change words on your stones if needed. Then
try telling it to a second person, perhaps to your
father.

7. Another way to review the kingdoms is to make
a photocopy of the dream image and cut off the
labels. Then see if you can label it from memory.
Can you tell how each kingdom was conquered
by the next?

8. If you have in your notebook the written sum-
maries of the early world and of Israel, you could
try to finish your history of the world by writing
a summary of the Gentile kingdoms. A summary
only needs to tell briefly how each kingdom followed the one before. It does not need a lot of
details.

Chapter 3—Sample Answers

1. Babylon, Persia, Greece, Rome
2. Nebuchadnezzar, Belshazzar, Daniel, handwriting, riverbed
3. Cyrus, Jews return, Xerxes, Themistocles, Athens, Sparta, Battle of Salamis
4. Alexander the Great, Europe, Asia, Africa, King Darius, Persian Gates
5. Julius Caesar, Antony, Cleopatra, Caesar Augustus, Christ, Eastern and Western Empires, broken pieces

The Kingdom of Christ

4

Directions: Read here the world's future history, which only the Bible can tell. Then try the notebook assignment either by itself or added to assignment 8 from the last chapter.

The ending of the story. The last part of Nebuchadnezzar's image was the toes made of iron and clay. We now live in the days of those toes. Here is what the Bible says will happen then.

> **Daniel 2**:34   ...a stone was cut out without hands, which smote the image upon his feet *that were* of iron and clay, and brake them to pieces.
> 35   Then was the iron, the clay, the brass, the silver, and the gold, broken to pieces together, and became like the chaff of the summer threshingfloors; and the wind carried them away, that no place was found for them: and the stone that smote the image became a great mountain, and filled the whole earth.
> 44   And in the days of these kings shall the God of heaven set up a kingdom, which shall never be destroyed:

and the kingdom shall not be left to other people, *but* it shall break in pieces and consume all these kingdoms, and it shall stand for ever.

45 Forasmuch as thou sawest that the stone was cut out of the mountain without hands, and that it brake in pieces the iron, the brass, the clay, the silver, and the gold; the great God hath made known to the king what shall come to pass hereafter: and the dream is certain, and the interpretation thereof sure.

Zechariah 14:9a And the LORD shall be king over all the earth:

The stone not cut by man that crushed the whole image stands for Jesus Christ. The mountain that fills the earth stands for the kingdom God will set up. It shall never be destroyed, but shall last forever.

The world has seen practically all of the image—from the gold downward through silver, brass, iron, and clay. That tells us that the end times are near. All who belong to Christ are now waiting to see Him come, to see the stone that will smash the image, smash the troubled and sinful nations and kings. The glorious kingdom of Jesus, the totally righteous King, will then fill the whole earth.

For Your Notebook • • • • • • • • • • • •

1. If you did assignment 8 in the last chapter, try adding a final paragraph that tells this future history. That can take just one or two sentences. Or tell this future history by itself.

History Dating

Directions for this chapter: The first four chapters gave the sweep of history from the creation of the world all the way to Christ's kingdom. They are best studied consecutively to take full advantage of that connected look at history. This chapter now can be used differently. It shows what is wrong with dating schemes in most history books, and shows how to use the Bible as a more dependable dating tool. You can select any portion you want at any time you want and in any order you want. History buffs may like to do all sections for an in-depth unit on history dating. Sample answers for sections that need them are at the end of the chapter.

HOW DATING WENT WRONG

Directions: This first portion explains dating problems that are seldom mentioned in schoolbooks. Follow-up activities are suggested after each sub-section, and independent students can probably do most of them on their own, although it would be a good idea to share some of their learnings with the family.

Egypt dating problems. Most books are quite wrong on the chronology of ancient history, and this began with Egypt. Here is the story of how we arrived at this mixed-up history.

The mix-up began mostly with the famous name of Manetho. He was an Egyptian historian of Greek times who wrote out long lists of pharaohs from all of Egypt's history. People assume that he had access to temple records in Egypt. Unfortunately, we do not have Manetho's original writings, but only later quotations from him by Greek writers, as often is the case with ancient writings. Greek historians did not fully agree on their interpretations of Manetho so we have different versions of his list.

In the 1800s, archeology came into vogue and scholars began reading hieroglyphics on Egyptian monuments and trying to identify each king that Manetho listed. That was difficult because the kings often had multiple names, multiple kings had the same name, co-reigns such as a son reigning with his ill father were not clear, inscriptions of kings sometimes were erased or changed by successors, and inscriptions often were damaged and incomplete. In this complex setting, various scholars made various lists. The greatest problem was that Manetho did not say what kings might be concurrent, reigning at the same time but in different parts of Egypt.

Historians never reached full agreement, but a dominant chronology became standard fare in schoolbooks and other history books. Throughout the 1900s archeologists uncovered more information and eventually realized that the standard chronology was too long, 400 to 600 years longer than it should be. Some then tried to shorten the chronology by figuring out which were competing concurrent kings or sub-kings rather than the main king of Egypt. In recent years several Christian authors tried to match Egyptian history with the Bible (see Bibliography). All these scholars agree that Egypt's history must be shortened by several centuries but they do not agree on the details of how and where to do it.

Because Egypt's history is too long, the history of all other Mediterranean and Middle East areas are long also because they are all tied to Egypt. For instance, your books are likely to mention a "dark age" in Greece, a period that produces no archeological evidence. Old Greece disappears from sight and then reappears centuries later with the same language and same pottery, a strange anomaly that historians cannot explain. Homer's account of the Trojan War was said to have been passed down orally through those centuries and then put into writing. Can you believe that? But the dark-age gap disappears once we shorten the history. (This dark age is in BC times; it is not the AD Middle Ages that are sometimes called the Dark Ages.)

In summary, historians made Egypt's history too long. Then all other Mediterranean history became misdated too because people tried to match everything with Egypt. This is probably the main reason for the history mix-up we have today. The following sections explain attempts, mostly unsuccessful, to straighten out the dating.

Follow-up • • • • • • • • • • • • • • •

1. Try to explain to someone how Egypt's history dating came to be several centuries too long.
2. Check any history books in your house to see how certain they sound about the date of particular pharaohs or of Homer.

(Possible answers are given at the end of this chapter.)

Sothic dating problems. One theory of what the Egyptians believed is that when the star Sothis (Sirius) rose just before the sun, the people celebrated their New Year. If that happened when the annual Nile flooding began, it was a special year. As the years went by, this Sothic rising slipped later and later in the year because the Egyptians had no leap year to keep things on schedule. Thus it was 1460 years before the Nile flooding and Sothic rising coincided again. (We don't have to believe that the farmers planted off season until the calendar got back on track. Farmers were smarter than that.)

Scientists assumed that ancient Egyptians did not know enough astronomy or mathematics to calculate that Sothic period, so they must have done it by observation. Only a scientist could think up a theory like that. We ordinary readers think it incredible that one morning someone would exclaim, "Look, Sothis is rising with the sun and the flooding is starting. This is exactly one thousand four hundred sixty years since the last time this happened." After several such observations Egyptians supposedly discovered the Sothic period. A by-product of this theory is that it needs a long prehistory of Egypt to allow for the observations. Another problem is that before the Sodom destruction Egypt probably did not need the Nile flooding anyway, because in those days it was like the "garden of the Lord," according to the Bible (Genesis 13:10).

Some scholars used this Sothic system to figure out dates for beginning and ending the period of Hyksos foreign rulers in Egypt. Their calculations left only 200 years for the Hyksos and many scholars thought that was too short a time. So they said the ending date of the Hyksos must be in the following Sothic period, a full 1460 years later. This battle between the short chronology and the long chronology continued until the death of one leading scholar; then the short chronology won. And yet, incredibly, historians held on to their theory of Sothic dating.

Other problems with Sothic dating include whether Sirius is actually the star referred to, what latitude or city was used for observing the rising, and what is the correct interpretation of ancient documents referring to Sothis. But the aura of astronomy surrounds this dating and many books use it. Others reject it completely.

Follow-up • • • • • • • • • • • • • • • •

1. Try to explain briefly what a Sothic period is.
2. See what your history books might say about the Sothic period. Indexes at the back of books are a fast way to find this.

Archeology dating problems. The system of referring to a Stone Age and to Copper, Bronze, and Iron Ages was developed from the study of Palestine, so it works only in that area. If a bronze item is found elsewhere, say Europe or Egypt for instance, that does not mean its time matches bronze items in Palestine. Moreover, the system cannot produce actual dates, but only a sequence. It says that the bronze items were made before iron items, but it does not say when the bronze items were made. Many scholars would like to do away with the whole system but they say they are stuck with it. It is in so many books now that they cannot abandon it.

Archeologists digging at Jericho have found walls fallen and undermined at their base as if by an earthquake. They find burned debris inside the city, in some places as much as two feet deep. They see that it was not a small village, but a city of 20,000. Ai, also, was completely destroyed as were a number of other Palestinian cities. These were not destroyed by a natural catastrophe and then rebuilt by the same people with the same culture, but they were invaded or destroyed and then inhabited with a new culture. All these findings exactly fit the Bible history and could easily be closely dated by using the Bible as the dating tool.

But archeologists use their other tools instead. They try to date Jericho by copper or bronze artifacts or by pottery types. Then they try to match those with a particular Egyptian king that they dated by other means. Problems pile one upon another, but the archeologists cling to their dating theories anyway, hoping that someday they will work out the puzzle. The Bible solves the puzzle: these Palestinian cities were destroyed in Joshua's time, and we can date Joshua fairly closely.

Follow-up ● ● ● ● ● ● ● ● ● ● ● ● ● ●

1. See what your history books say about the Stone Age or one of the other archeological ages.

Astronomy dating problems. Astronomers can predict eclipses accurately, so this sounds like the ultimate solution to dating problems. Just let astronomers calculate backward with the same accuracy. All we need are ancient documents that mention eclipses in connection with particular events; then let astronomers do their work.

But ancient writers were not always clear as to whether an eclipse was full or partial, what latitude it was viewed from, or even whether it was an eclipse of the moon or of the sun. We also need a proven connection between our calendar and the calendar of the time and place in question. And we need a correct interpretation of the ancient document. If the Bible says the sun went down at noon, did it go down at noon or should we interpret that to mean an eclipse?

And this ultimate question: Has something catastrophic happened to Earth's rotation so that all astronomical calculations before such a time are useless anyway? Bishop Ussher wrote in his scholarly *The Annuls of
the World*, "...from the evening of Wednesday, February
26, in the year 747 BC, all astronomers unanimously
start the calendar of Nabonassar." This universal change
could not have been a decree of Nabonassar, but had to
be a change in the skies that caused people everywhere
in the world to revise their calendars.

To match that calendar change with the Bible, the
most likely time was the "earthquake" of Amos 1:1. The
Hebrew word *raash* found in this verse is more than an
earthquake. One way to see that, even in English, is to
skim down through that chapter and into the next and
see how extensive was the destruction of fire. Another
place to see it is in Isaiah 1:7-9, where the prophet
preached to the people immediately after the *raash*.
That destruction and two sundial changes that followed
periodically could have been caused by a recurring comet passing by. Such a change in Earth's rotation would
render useless all astronomical retrocalculations before
that date.

Follow-up • • • • • • • • • • • • •

1. Tell at least one reason why astronomy seems
   like a good tool to help with dating.
2. Tell at least one reason why astronomy might
   not work as a dating tool.
3. Skim-read through Amos 1:1 to 2:5 and Isaiah
   1:7-9 and underline the word *fire* and any other
   words that indicate destruction after the *raash*.
4. Read about sundial changes for Hezekiah and
   his father Ahaz. See Isaiah 38:7-8. More pieces
   of the stories are in Isaiah 7:11-12 and 2 Kings

20:8-11. Can you figure out how long a time ten degrees is?

Chemical dating problems. Carbon-14 decay is the method commonly used for historical dating of just a few thousand years. This measures the amount of carbon-14 remaining in wood or other organic matter obtained from an archeological site. Theoretically, knowing the rate of carbon-14 decay once the tree has died should let us calculate how old its wood is.

This method has had detractors from its start. We must *assume* that we know the amount of carbon-14 in the carbon dioxide of the atmosphere at the time and place to be dated, and we must *assume* that the intensity of cosmic radiation, which causes the decay, has remained constant. When scientists suspected that it was not constant, they adjusted their figures by matching with a system of tree-ring dating, which has problems of its own.

Another type of problem occurs in dating ruins of a building. Is the resulting date close to the time the building was constructed? Or was that timber felled long before? Was it, perhaps, even reused from a previous building? With various problems, scientists often cannot agree on how to interpret their lab results.

An example of this is when they are trying to date an archeological layer called Iron Age I and another layer called Iron Age II, but disagree on what the dates should be. Some say Iron Age I matches Solomon's time, and that would show Solomon to be a poor king. Others say Iron Age II matches Solomon's time and that would show him to be a rich king. We know from the Bible that Solomon was rich, so here the Bible is a better dating tool than carbon-14. From what archeologists call Iron Age II there are remains of rich palaces, of stables, and of other artifacts that fit what we know of Solomon's kingdom. Those who date Iron Age I to Solomon argue that the Bible is wrong, that the Jews built up their history to be greater than it actually was.

The carbon-14 dating system, similar to the archeological-age system, is unable to show *absolute* dates. But in general it helps to show *relative* dates. That is, it shows which of two artifacts is younger and which is older.

Dating systems from other chemical elements give far older dates so they do not work at all for history. People use them for the millions of years of prehistory that they believe in.

Follow-up ● ● ● ● ● ● ● ● ● ● ● ● ● ●

1. Try to describe briefly how carbon-14 dating works.
2. Name at least one problem with carbon-14 dating.

Summary of dating problems. Manetho's lists of Egyptian kings turned out not to be the foundation for ancient chronology. Archeological ages do not determine absolute dates, only relative dating, and separately for separate areas. Astronomy inspires awe, but is challenged on several fronts. Chemical dating has numerous problems. Those four dating systems are the ones commonly used in books on ancient history—that is, the history before about 750 BC, most of the Old Testament times. Often the books do not explain which method they use to derive their dates. And sometimes they just copy somebody who copied somebody else.

If you try to build your own timeline for ancient history before about 750 BC, you will soon find that books differ and that you have taken on an impossible job. You could get further by using the Bible as your main dating tool. Try to match history with the Bible, and not the other way around. The following sections offer some help for using the Bible to date history.

Follow-up ● ● ● ● ● ● ● ● ● ● ● ● ● ●

1. Find in your history books one or two dates earlier than 750 BC. Does a book tell that it used Egypt or archeological ages or astronomy or chemistry to arrive at the date? Or does it not specify at all where the date came from?

HOW TO DATE THE OLD TESTAMENT

Directions: This section lists seven historical Bible periods and shows how to determine the number of years in each. Follow-up for these seven periods can take considerable family Bible study time, or independent students could work on their own. Many students can independently work the graph project that follows the seven periods.

1. Adam to the Flood. From the genealogy in Genesis 5:3-32, list the age of each father at the birth of his son. For Noah, list 600 years because that is how old he was when the Flood came (Genesis 7:6). This totals to 1656 years for the pre-Flood history. Save this list as a good start for the project on graphing the patriarch life spans that follows these seven periods.

2. Flood to Canaan. Use Genesis 11:10-26. Arphaxad was born two years after the Flood, so list those two years and then the age of each patriarch at the birth of his son. For Terah, do not list the 70 years mentioned in verse 26. That is when his first son was born. Do a bit of arithmetic with Genesis 12:4 and Acts 7:4 to figure out that Abram was born when Terah was 130 years old. On the list show only 75 of Abram's years—his age when he entered Canaan. Add these figures for a total of 427 years from the Flood to Canaan. For those centuries the Bible tells only a brief history of the tower of Babel and the dispersion of peoples. Secular books tell about early civilization in Sumer.

3. Sojourn. According to Galatians 3:17, the sojourn extends from the time Abram entered Canaan and received the covenant to the giving of the law at the Exodus. The verse says it was 430 years total, including the sojourn both in Canaan and in Egypt. Some books use Exodus 12:40 to say the people were in Egypt 430 years, but that verse only says they *sojourned* that long, not that they lived in Egypt that long. Moses was only the fourth generation from Jacob (or third generation through his mother's line). That fits a 215-year span in Egypt rather than 430 years. The sojourn is said to be 400 years when it begins with Abram's "seed" Isaac, and 430 years when it begins with Abram's covenant. Use the 430 year total for your list.

4. Exodus to the Temple. 1 Kings 6:1 clearly specifies 480 years for this eventful period. It extends to the fourth year of Solomon's reign when he celebrated the Temple groundbreaking. History during these centuries includes the wilderness wanderings, Joshua's conquest, the judges, and the reigns of Saul and David, 480 years in all.

At the end of the same chapter, 1 Kings 6:38, we read that Solomon was 7 years in building the Temple.

If we add on these 7 years we find the striking information that the Temple was finished in the 3000th year of
the world. At this time the glory of the Lord filled the
Temple.

   5. *Kings of Judah*. It is easier to list the kings of Judah than the kings of Israel, so that's what we do next.
Begin the list with the 36 remaining years of Solomon's
forty-year reign that were not counted in the previous
period. Then list the reigns of each king from Rehoboam
down through Zedekiah. Starting with 2 Chronicles
12:13, you can find most of them near the beginnings of
following chapters.

   A good family activity is to have different children
make the same list but use 1 Kings 14 to 2 Kings 24,
and compare with the Chronicles list. Both lists should
total the same. Subtract 4 years for a co-reign of Joram
(Jehoram) with his father Jehoshaphat. This is a complicated calculation from 1 Kings 22:41,43; 2 Kings 3:1,
8:16,25; and 9:29—further complicated by the fact that
there were two king Jehorams. Some people postulate
more co-reigns in an effort to match the Bible with
dates from secular history. Here with the one co-reign,
the total is 426 years.

   6. *Captivity*. The captivity began in the eleventh year
of Zedekiah. That's when Nebucadnezzar of Babylon
destroyed Jerusalem, burning the wall and palaces and
Temple, and killing and capturing many people. We read
about this in 2 Kings 25 and 2 Chronicles 36:11-21.
There had been previous partial captivities of the Jews
and previous forcings of their kings to submit to Babylon, but with this invasion there was no more kingdom
of Judah. It was final.

Jeremiah (29:10) prophesied that after 70 years the Lord would bring the Jews back to their land. Isaiah (44:28) actually named King Cyrus before he was born, and said that he would decree that Jerusalem be rebuilt. It happened just as prophesied. The last three verses of II Chronicles tells of the decree, and Ezra and Nehemiah tell about returning to the land. Both Ezra 2 and Nehemiah 7 list the first group to return, under the leadership of Zerubbabel. There were 42,360 men plus their servants and maids and singers. That could equal 100,000 people altogether. Later, some smaller groups of people returned.

Chronologers do not all agree on the beginning and ending of this captivity. Some begin at one of the earlier partial captivities instead of the final one. And some end it at a later partial return instead of the first and largest return. These and other differences in details do not make a significant difference in the grand total of years for the Old Testament. Here, we add 70 years for the period of captivity.

7. Daniel's 69 "weeks." In Daniel 9:25 we find the word weeks or sevens, depending on the translation used. Here it means weeks of years. Multiply the sixty-two sevens and separately multiply the seven sevens. Add those, and it totals 483 years—the time period from the end of captivity until Christ.

Summary of Old Testament times. Here is a summary list of the Bible periods described above.

1656	years from creation to the Flood
427	years from the Flood to Canaan
430	years sojourn in Canaan and Egypt
480	years from the Exodus to Temple ground-breaking
426	years of the kings of Judah
70	years captivity
483	years from the end of captivity to Christ
3972	total years from Adam to Christ

This total of 3972 in a round number is almost 4000 years of Old Testament history. Many chronologers want to come out with exactly 4000 years. Bishop Ussher, a scholarly chronologist of the 1600s, calculated exactly 4000 years from creation to the birth of Christ. Others calculate 4000 years to the death of Christ. Some use Assyrian dates for part of the time instead of staying only with the Bible. Thus they differ over details, some of which are mentioned above.

It is good for students, especially future historians, to realize that not all history problems are solved yet, and there is work left for them to do.

Follow-up ● ● ● ● ● ● ● ● ● ● ● ● ● ●

1. Make a wall chart or notebook page showing the seven Bible periods listed above. Draw it out like a timeline if you wish. Add details and dress it up in any way you like.

2. For family devotions or Bible study take one or more days for each Bible period described in the sections above. Read the Scriptures and do the calculations suggested in some sections. This

will help show that the Bible is careful and accurate history.

Graphing the patriarch life spans. This project will take some time and careful work. It is for serious history buffs.

1) Look in Genesis 5 and make a list of the names from Adam to Noah. You should have ten in all. After each name write the age he was when his son was born, and write his age at death. Since Shem was the second son of Noah, you need to use also verses 7:6 and 11:10 and do a bit of arithmetic to figure out that Noah was 502 at Shem's birth. You also need verses 9:28-29 to find Noah's age at death.

2) Next, look in chapter 11 and continue your list from Shem down to Abram. They are all easy until you come to Abram. Use Genesis 11:32, 12:4, and Acts 7:4, and do the arithmetic to show that Abram was born when Terah was 130. Abram, like Shem, was not the firstborn son.

3) From your list, construct a bar graph. List the names down the left side of the graph. With graph paper you can let one square equal 100 years or any number you choose. With plain paper, let one-fourth inch equal 100 years or any number you choose, depending on how large a chart you wish to make. Refer to your list, and to the right of Adam's name draw a line the length of his life. To the right of Seth's name start a line at Adam's 130th year and draw the length of Seth's life. Continue this way for the whole graph. Begin like this.

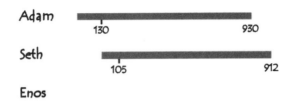

Adam

130   930

Seth

105   912

Enos

When you finish, look at verse 7:6 and draw a vertical line to show when the Flood happened. You can read interesting facts from this graph. Which people could talk to Adam in person? Which man died the very year of the Flood? When did the life spans begin to get shorter? When did they get shorter again? You will have a valuable picture of the early years of the world.

Some history writers stretch more time into history by saying that the genealogies in Genesis 5 and 11 are not literally accurate. They say there could be extra generations not mentioned. There is no Bible reason for doing this; their reason is that other books say history is longer, so they are trying to make the Bible history longer too. After you read Genesis 5 and 11, what do you think? Do you find a good place to insert extra years?

Follow-up ● ● ● ● ● ● ● ● ● ● ● ● ●

1. To make this eye-opening graph, follow steps 1, 2, and 3 as described above. Show your graph to adult visitors. They will be amazed to see things they never learned in Sunday school.

HOW TO USE BC DATES

Directions: Follow-up for this section on reading BC dates requires teacher and student working together, ideally repeating the quiz for several weeks.

Reading BC dates. BC stands for "Before Christ." To think about these tricky dates, you have to put your mind into reverse and count backward. That might be easy enough for round numbers like 1900 BC, 2000 BC, 2100 BC, and so forth. But now think 1923 BC. Is that before or after 1900 BC? That becomes so tricky that even adult history writers sometimes get it wrong. To visualize this, draw a timeline and number it backward for BC dates. Most historians agree that Christ was probably born in 3 or 4 BC; the Romans missed a bit when they first made the AD calendar.

People may also get it wrong with ordinal numbers, words that tell the order of dates—*first* century, *second* century, and so forth. Are dates like 290 BC or 246 BC in the second century? No, they are in the third. You can illustrate this on your timeline. You will see that the first century begins at 1 and continues to 99 or to 100. Second century dates are in the 100s. Third century dates are in the 200s.

Modern books often use BCE, which stands for "Before Common Era." They do that because they do not want to use the name of Christ. Common Era, CE, then, stands for AD times. You may occasionally run into BP, which means "Before Present." People sometimes use this with chemical datings. It means an object dated that number of years before the lab dated it. We are left to do the arithmetic and translate that BP date into a calendar year.

It takes practice and concentrated thinking to use BC dates correctly. Here are five types of questions to help master BC thinking. Repeat the full set every week or so for a while, changing the numbers each time.

Follow-up • • • • • • • • • • • • • • • •
1. Tell (or write) a date in the fourth century BC.
2. Tell a date early in the fourth century BC.
3. Tell a date late in the fourth century.
4. In what century is 1160 BC?
5. Write this BC date: 412. Write this AD date: 1492.

Directions: Most students can independently do the follow-up for this next section on converting dates. But the concept is rather complicated, and family discussion could help to clarify it.

Converting to BC dates. In the Old Testament we can count the years precisely up to Solomon and approximately after that, as long as we count years of the world, moving forward from creation. The Flood came precisely in the year 1656 AM (Latin *anno mundi*, year of the world). All the history that we can dig up happened after that Flood date. The garden of Eden and other pre-Flood places are completely destroyed.

Since most books use BC dates, we need a way to convert, and we do this by subtracting AM dates from 4000. Subtracting the Flood date of 1656 from 4000 gives us a date of 2344 BC. This is approximate because the 4000 total is not precise. But this approximate Flood date is highly useful. For easy memory, you can round it off to 2350 BC.

Most books do not acknowledge the Flood and just begin history with the rebuilding of civilization afterward. When you read about Mesopotamia or Egypt or anything that came after the Flood you sometimes see dates older than 2350 BC. In fact you usually see dates older than that. To match history with the Bible you can begin marking up your history books to change those dates. Or if you are not a book marker, you can at least say to yourself that a book is using one of the problematic dating systems. It does not match the Bible.

Another important date is the Exodus. It is precisely 2513 AM. Rounding off and subtracting from 4000 gives a date of 1500 BC. It seems that more books get that right than the Flood date. That Exodus date marks the fall of the Middle Kingdom of Egypt.

Abram was born about 2000 BC, halfway between creation and Christ. That date sometimes is useful. If you know that something happened before or after Abraham, then you can decide whether the dates in a history book are correct.

Those dates for the early world are enough for practically all of us. If we ever want more we can look them up on our Bible charts and convert. The chart below shows rounded BC dates.

1AM		1656AM	2008AM	2513AM		about 4000AM
Creation		Flood	Abraham	Exodus		Christ
4000BC		2350BC	2000BC	1500BC		about 3BC

Follow-up ● ● ● ● ● ● ● ● ● ● ● ● ●

1. Draw this timeline for a wall chart to remind you of the order of events. Learn the rounded BC dates.
2. Test yourself. Can you sketch this timeline from memory?

Directions: This section on reading history books can be worked independently or as family discussion. The whole family can help watch in the future for dating examples in books.

Reading history books. The following passages are quoted from typical history books. How do these statements match or mismatch with Bible history? With a little practice, you can learn to evaluate history books, comparing each with the Bible.

1. Prehistory makes up more than 95 percent of our time on this planet, yet history, the remaining 5 percent, makes up at least 95 percent of most history books.

2. The earliest people lived as nomads, hunting animals and gathering wild plants. The change to a settled, agricultural way of life was a gradual one, occurring in different places at different times.

3. Farming probably began in the Middle East in about 9000 BC in an area known as the Fertile Crescent. As people adopted farming, they began to build permanent settlements. One of the best known is Jericho, which had about 2000 people by 8000 BC. It was destroyed in 7000 BC and later rebuilt.

4. The earliest pottery from northeast China is about 9,000 years old while that found in south China may be as old as 10,000 BP [Before Present, which equals about 8,000 BC].

5. In Egypt we are faced with a gap of nearly three millennia in the archeological record, but Neolithic [New Stone Age] sites do appear after 6000 BC.

6. These findings in Egypt are not the products of autochthonous [self] development, but have all the earmarks of having been introduced from outside suddenly. Orthodox Egyptologists do not supply us with a convincing explanation for the sudden beginning of civilization in Egypt.

7. These Middle Kingdom texts with magical curse formulas must be dated about 1850 to 1750 BC.

8. Greek civilization ended abruptly around 1250 BC and a "dark age" followed until the rise of the brilliant classical Greek civilization in 500 BC.

Find another dating quote from a book around your house. Try to compare it with the Bible.

Chapter 5—Sample Answers
Egypt Dating Problems

1. We do not have original pharaoh lists, only quotes from parts of Manetho's list, and Manetho lived long after the Egyptian pharaohs. It is hard to match those names with names found on monument inscriptions.
2. Answers will vary. Books give different dates and may not explain how the dates were obtained.

Sothic Dating Problems

1. The period of time between the rising of the star Sothis with the sun until the next time it rises with the sun. That was 1460 years.
2. Books that mention Sothic dating usually accept the system as scientific truth. Some recent books discuss problems with Sothic dating.
3. Ten degrees equals 40 minutes. One way to calculate this is to divide 360 degrees by 24, the hours in a day. This shows that 15 degrees equals 1 hour. Thus 10 degrees is two-thirds of that or 40 minutes.

Archeology Dating Problems

1. Books that mention Stone Age usually accept it as being useful for dating.

Astronomy Dating Problems

1. Astronomy is precise and mathematical.
2. If there was a change in Earth's rotation, that would disrupt mathematical calculations. People may misinterpret ancient documents about eclipses.

Chemical Dating Problems

1. It measures the amount of carbon-14 in an artifact and figures from that how long it had been decaying.
2. We can't be sure the decay rate was constant. We can't be sure of the starting amount.

Graphing the Patriarch Life Spans

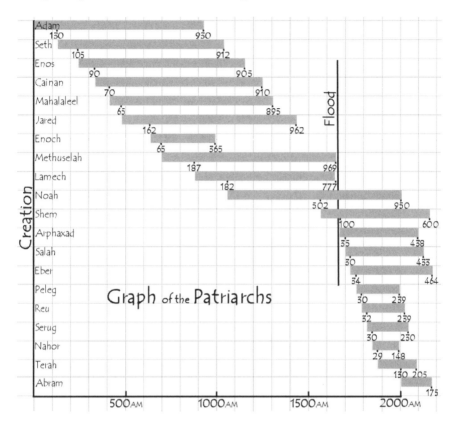

Graph of the Patriarchs

How to Use BC Dates
1. Any date in the 300s. The first century is years 1 to 99; the second is the 100s, etc.
2. Example: 398 BC.
3. Example: 304 BC.
4. Twelfth.
5. 412 BC and AD 1492. Standard usage is that BC follows the numerals and AD precedes them.

Reading History Books
1. Prehistory refers to the theoretical time before writing or civilizations. It is unbiblical to postulate thousands of years for mankind to develop into true humans like Adam. Adam could write, and we have his account of the Garden of Eden.

2. This is simply a theory that fits with evolution. If Noah and family began hunting immediately they could have wiped out animals before they had much chance to multiply. The Bible records that Noah had a vineyard; he was a farmer, not a hunter. Adam, too, was a farmer.
3. The area for beginning agriculture fits the Bible; it would be the new start after the Flood. Jericho probably was destroyed more than once. One destruction would be Joshua's, but all the dates here are far too old for the Bible.
4. Both dates are too old for the Bible. This does not say how the dates were derived.
5. A hypothetical gap appears from trying to match findings with dates of so-called Old Stone Age and New Stone Age. Also, 6000 BC is not a biblical date; it would be older than the Flood, and even older than the Earth itself.
6. The sudden beginning is easily explained by people moving down to Egypt after the Babel judgment.
7. These dates could be correct. The Middle Kingdom collapsed with the Exodus at about 1500 BC and the dates given are about 300 years before that.
8. This dark age—not the Middles Ages of AD times—is a result of trying to match Greek archeology with the too-long Egyptian history. If they get the dates right the dark age disappears.

Annotated Bibliography

Matching Chronology with the Bible ● ● ● ● ●

Centuries of Darkness by Peter James and four other archeologists. These scientists studied archeological evidences of Greeks and other Mediterranean peoples, dating them independently of Egypt. They concluded that the traditionally posited dark age (a BC dark age, not the AD Middle Age) was not there; it should be closed up and the history shortened by several centuries. They further concluded that the current dating problems must have come from an incorrect chronology of Egypt. Adult level study. (Rutgers University Press, 1993.)

Chronology of the Old Testament by Floyd Nolan Jones. An excellent study into the details of chronology from a biblical viewpoint. It solves many chronology problems of the Bible, and discusses problems with the Assyrian king lists that many chronologers use. For late teens and adult. (KingsWord Press, 1999).

Pharaohs and Kings: A Biblical Quest by David M. Rohl. The easiest reading book in this list, by a scholar experienced in the archeology of Egypt. Rohl works to match Egyptian history with the Bible, thereby juggling the traditional dates for some of the pharaohs. He agrees with Velikovsky and Josephus and some others that Tutimaos (Dudimose) probably was the pharaoh of the Exodus. He tells a fascinating story of identifying Joseph's tomb. Teens and adult. (Crown, 1995.)

Solving the Exodus Mystery by Ted T. Stewart. This reworks Egyptian history more thoroughly than the two books above, and differs from both of them, as well as from the earlier Velikovsky and Courville studies, on how to rearrange the pharaohs. Stewart particularly tries to identify the pharoahs of Abraham's and Joseph's times and of Moses and the Exodus. Covers the period from Abraham to the Exodus. Ages late teens and adult. (Biblemart.com, 1999.)

The Annals of the World by James Ussher, revised and updated by Larry and Marion Pierce. This 1654 masterpiece of historical chronology covers time from creation to AD 70. Ussher's dates were commonly used in Bible notes until the belief in an "old Earth" became the fashion. The Pierces have translated this, and in footnotes added newer information that was not available to Ussher. This large expensive book is for reference. Bible chronologists may differ from this, but only on minor details. (Master Books, 2003.)

The Exodus Problem and its Ramifications, Volumes 1 and 2 by Donovan A. Courville. These two books present a detailed study of Egypt's pharaohs and Assyrian kings and other history, trying to match everything with the Bible, thus shortening Egypt's history by several hundred years, as all the revisionists do. But this massive reworking of Egypt's history differs from all other Egyptologists. It has only two kingdoms of ancient Egypt rather than three, and thus only one intermediate period. Courville approved of Velikovsky's work back in the days when few scholars did, agreeing that astronomical causes reasonably explain upheavals in Bible times and that various scientific dating systems have numerous problems. For adult serious readers of Egyptian history. (Out of print, Challenge Books, Loma Linda, CA, 1971.)

Earth Catastrophes ● ● ● ● ● ● ● ● ● ● ● ●

Ages in Chaos by Immanuel Velikovsky. This book begins with the Exodus and moves on to the time of Israel's kings and prophets, matching historical happenings with Bible history. This was a best seller with the general public, but scientists of the time opposed and repressed it, as it tampered with their Egyptian history and it treated the Bible as real history. Today there is renewed interest and demand for this and other of Velikovsky's books. (Rare and out of print, first published 1953, reprinted 1973 to 1990, Macdonald & Co., Ltd. London.)

Earth in Upheaval by Immanuel Velikovsky. A study of catastrophic upheavals in Earth's history that are evident by geology and paleontology, avoiding any reference to the Bible and to other ancient literature, traditions, and folklore. (Rare and out of print, 1955 Simon & Schuster.)

Worlds in Collision by Immanuel Velikovsky. Centers on the Exodus and its following upheavals, using both science and the Old Testament and other literature from around the world. Velikovsky, a Jew, first turned to this study because he believed the Genesis account. He lived and wrote before the modern creation movement, so he was not a young earther. Nevertheless, his writings help the creationist view today. (Rare and out of print, 1950 Simon & Schuster.)

Early History of the World • • • • • • • • •

Adam and His Kin by Ruth Beechick. Narrative history from Adam to Abram. This story form connects events and provides insights beyond the typical Sunday school lessons on this history. Ages about 10 and up. (www.mottmedia.com)

Genesis: Finding Our Roots by Ruth Beechick. Teaches many details such as who wrote the first book in the world, and where the giants came from. Provides a good understanding of the times from Adam to Abram. This teaches all important Bible doctrines right from the first eleven chapters of the Bible, thus providing students with a clear and solid basis for a biblical worldview. This can qualify as an ancient history course or a Bible literature course for high school. Hardcover, full color. Ages about 12 and up. (www.mottmedia.com)

Index